everything lost

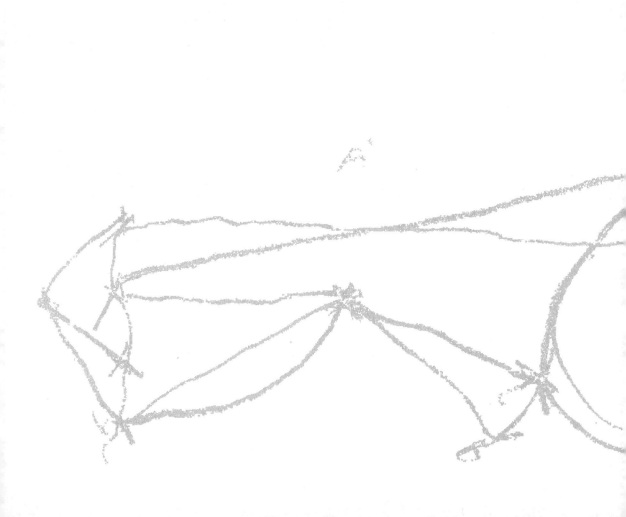

everything lost

THE LATIN AMERICAN NOTEBOOK OF
WILLIAM S. BURROUGHS

REVISED EDITION

GENERAL EDITORS
Geoffrey D. Smith and John M. Bennett

VOLUME EDITOR
Oliver Harris

THE OHIO STATE UNIVERSITY PRESS / COLUMBUS

Library of Congress Cataloging-in-Publication Data
Names: Burroughs, William S., 1914–1997, author. | Smith, Geoffrey D. (Geoffrey Dayton),
    1948– editor. | Bennett, John M., editor. | Harris, Oliver (Oliver C. G.), editor.
Title: Everything lost : the Latin American notebook of William S. Burroughs / editors Geoffrey
    D. Smith, John M. Bennett, and Oliver Harris.
Description: Revised edition. | Columbus : The Ohio State University Press, [2017] | Includes
    bibliographical references.
Identifiers: LCCN 2016053674 | ISBN 9780814253830 (pbk. ; alk. paper) | ISBN 0814253830
    (pbk. ; alk. paper)
Subjects: LCSH: Burroughs, William S., 1914–1997—Notebooks, sketchbooks, etc. | Burroughs,
    William S., 1914–1997—Travel—Latin America.
Classification: LCC PS3552.U75 E63 2017 | DDC 813/.54—dc23
LC record available at https://lccn.loc.gov/2016053674

Cover design by Christian Fuenfhausen
Type set in Adobe Rotis
Text design by Jennifer Shoffey Forsythe and Juliet Williams

♾ The paper used in this publication meets the minimum requirements of the American National Standard for Information Sciences—Permanance of Paper for Printed Library Materials. ANSI Z39.49-1992.

9 8 7 6 5 4 3 2 1

contents

ACKNOWLEDGMENTS   vii

INTRODUCTION BY OLIVER HARRIS   ix

COMMENTS ON THE TEXT BY GEOFFREY D. SMITH   xxvii

NOTEBOOK FACSIMILE   1

FAIR COPY   105

TRANSCRIPT   123

ABOUT THE EDITORS   151

acknowledgments

First and foremost, the editors wish to thank James Grauerholz, literary executor of the William S. Burroughs estate, for permission to publish this seminal holograph notebook. We also thank James for his stalwart support over the years. The Ohio State University Press has been a strong advocate for this project and, in particular, Sandy Crooms, Senior Acquisitions Editor, Eugene O'Connor and Tara Cyphers, Managing Editors, and Jennifer Shoffey Forsythe and Juliet Williams, Designers and Typesetters, who have been unstinting in their efforts to bring this publication to fruition. Cover design by Christian Fuenfhausen. Each of the editors also thanks those family and friends who bear with our obsessions.

introduction

BY OLIVER HARRIS

The publication of a notebook written by William Burroughs in Latin America during July and August 1953 might seem a matter of some marginal interest, but appearances are deceptive and this is a rare object of four-fold significance.

Firstly, its content must make us revise and rethink Burroughs' biography at a key point early in his literary career. Biographers have been able to narrate his South American quest for *yagé* by drawing on his letters from this period—both those in *The Letters of William S. Burroughs, 1945–1959,* and the dozen attributed to his persona, William Lee, that appeared as "In Search of Yage" within *The Yage Letters.* But the focus of this notebook lies elsewhere and tells a very different story of Burroughs' life as it stood in late summer 1953. Secondly, there is the specific importance of the notebook form in Burroughs' development as a writer. This, the only surviving example, allows us to recognise for the first time the notebook's role in Burroughs' creative practice, as we see him working autobiographical fragments into the fabric of his fictional universe. We can now therefore also measure the notebook's genetic and formal relation to the creative use Burroughs was starting to make of his letters, a decisive factor in the evolution of *Naked Lunch.* Thirdly, the notebook provides striking, detailed revelations about the fluid state of Burroughs' manuscripts and the ways in which he reworked them. In particular, it offers primary evidence for a far more complex picture of how he wrote major parts of what became *Queer* and *The Yage Letters.* Finally, this notebook is a unique physical remnant, and it is its singularity as a material object that makes it so fitting to be the subject of this, the first facsimile edition of a text by William Burroughs.

To begin by expanding on this final point, *The Latin American Notebook of William S. Burroughs* marks an important advance in Burroughs textual scholarship and editing. It does so by building on two decades' of publications that have enlarged incrementally our knowledge of Burroughs' writing during the 1950s—starting with the release of *Queer* in 1985, followed by the *Interzone* collection (1989), *The Letters, 1945–1959* (1993), and three major new editions: *Naked Lunch: the restored text* (2003), edited by James Grauerholz and Barry Miles, and my own *Junky: the definitive text of "Junk"* (2003) and *The Yage Letters Redux* (2006). Shedding further light on Burroughs' foundational decade as a writer, the *Notebook* takes its place in this expansion of the scholarly field. But as an object it is entirely singular, which is why it is so appropriate that Geoffrey D. Smith and John M. Bennett should have assembled with such care this facsimile reproduction and transcription for The Ohio State University Press. For none of Burroughs' other manuscripts from this era have survived in complete form but exist only as pieces scattered across various archives—a state of disarray that reflects his lack of care as an archivist of his own material and the chaotic circumstances in which he wrote on his travels. In contrast, this notebook, the sole survivor from that past, retains a distinct physical existence whose appearance and particular feel is conveyed so well in facsimile. And so, from the opening page we immediately get an extraordinarily vivid picture of Burroughs himself, sitting alone in some dingy bar in the Peruvian coastal town of Talara, pencil in hand—his "5 P.M. rum" in the other—pressing his thoughts and observations onto the paper in his own, instantly recognisable style ("Got to watch drinking," he adds in parentheses, noting dryly, "I can black out on 4 drinks now").

The entries run from mid-July to early August 1953, and they fill out numerous minor gaps in the record of Burroughs' travels: as well as learning more about his stays in Panama and Mexico City, we now know of his stopovers in Talara, Guatemala City, and Tapachulla, and about his short trips to Vera Cruz, on the Gulf of Mexico, and to Mérida, on the Yucatan Peninsula. But the initial impression of a standard travel diary is misleading, and it soon becomes clear that Burroughs is using the notebook to sketch scenes that dramatize a critical moment in his life. A year that had begun with the inauguration of Eisenhower in Washington and the opening of *The Crucible* on Broadway, saw Burroughs depart Mexico City—since late 1949 his haven from Cold War America, but also the site of his blackest hour: the shooting of his wife, Joan—and start out, via a stopover in Miami, on his seven-month journey through the jungles of Colombia, Ecuador, and Peru. Burroughs would remain in exile for a quarter-of-a-century, dividing his time between Tangier, Paris, and London, but this was his one true expedition, and only in 1953 did he live and write constantly on the move. The *Notebook* begins on the last leg of the travels made familiar through *The Yage Letters,* and ends with Burroughs about to leave for New York and a long-awaited rendezvous with Allen Ginsberg. And yet, although his debut novel, *Junkie,* had just been published and although he had completed an adventure that would generate "an awful lot of copy" for future work,[1] the *Notebook* reveals a man contemplating dead-end despair and disaster, rather than anticipating any kind of success.

Some of the early sketches recall the vignettes of "In Search of Yage," and are written similarly in "a style which has the bitter irony of Daumier, the briefness of a Webern song."[2] But a more anguished and literally *ominous* element comes increasingly to the fore. Take his recollections of Lima, which run like a refrain through the *Notebook.* On the second page, Burroughs glumly notes, "Last few days in Lima. Cold and damp." Six pages later, after describing his arrival in Panama, he returns to "Last days in Lima," now reporting the "feeling of urgency" that makes him want to leave "at once." Thirty pages further on, these "last days" turn first into "a nightmare" and then an apocalyptic vision in the shape of a dream in which an "atomic cloud" spreads over the city. Drawn back to his memories, rewriting them as ever more sinister omens, Burroughs gives his last days in Lima an eschatological twist, literalising them as millennial end times.

Burroughs' vision of doom is developed further through a small range of specific cultural references. His allusions to country music ballads, which are predictably contemptuous of their sentimentality—"How could anyone be stupid enough to

---

1. Burroughs interviewed by Conrad Knickerbocker (1965), *The Paris Review Interviews,* edited by George Plimpton (New York: Viking, 1967), 77.
2. Donatella Manganotti, "The Final Fix," *Kulchur* 4, no.15 (Autumn 1964): 78.

enjoy that bleating, whining crap," he snarls of songs that include Hank Williams' posthumous hit, "Your Cheatin' Heart" (17)—also feed the sense of his isolation from contemporary America, and the blighted blandness of what he calls in a later entry "one of the most gruesome cultural straight jackets in history" (67). More significant (and surprising) is his quotation from Gustav Mahler's *Das Lied von der Erde* (83). Burroughs invokes the famous lyric, "Dark is life, dark is death," in the context of his preoccupation throughout the *Notebook* with individual and cultural processes of decay, aging, unfulfilled desire and death—and his despair at the poor compensations of art: "As though it made things any better to write about them." And finally, his theme is developed through four literary references that are easily missed—because such references aren't prominent in Burroughs' writing—but that are particularly resonant.

The first is to Kafka, by way of an allusion to his story "In the Penal Colony" (51), which would also figure in other contemporaneous writing.[3] Here, Burroughs identifies himself as an emotionally brutalized "Displaced Person," echoing his sense of isolated suffering, trapped in the straitjacket of American cultural values. The second, through references to Captain Ahab and the white whale (75, 83), is to Melville's *Moby Dick,* suggesting Burroughs had revised his verdict to Ginsberg back in April that his expedition had not been "Ahabesque" (*Letters* 157). Ginsberg's own understanding of why Burroughs invoked Melville is clear enough from the account he would give of his "Yage" manuscript in a letter to Malcolm Cowley that September, shortly after Burroughs had arrived in New York: "kind of an Ahab-quest; however survived."[4] Taking up the trajectory of a fateful imperial mission, the third significant literary allusion is to Joseph Conrad, invoked elliptically in one of the *Notebook's* final entries as a devastating summation of Burroughs' own journey into a heart of darkness (99):

Miami—

Panama—

---

3. See *The Letters of William S. Burroughs, 1945–1959* (New York: Viking, 1993), 140, and "Dream of the Penal Colony," in *Interzone* (New York: Viking, 1989), 43–46.

4. Ginsberg to Cowley, September 2, 1953 (Ginsberg Collection, Columbia University).

Colombia—

The horror

Again, Ginsberg fully understood, and in his letter to Cowley described Burroughs' "travels in Jungles and end-of-road-Conradian despair." The final literary reference in the *Notebook* is the most revelatory, and calls for more detailed attention.

Preceding one of his references to Captain Ahab, but without any evident context, Burroughs notes: "St. Perse. <u>This is Yage poetry</u>" (75). This is Burroughs' first recorded reference to St.-John Perse, pseudonym of the former high-ranking French diplomat Alexis Léger, recipient of the Nobel Prize in 1960. In the early 1960s Burroughs would refer to St.-Perse, together with Rimbaud, to identify the poetics of his cut-up experiments. This much earlier allusion in the *Notebook* is particularly relevant, for two related reasons. Firstly, there is Burroughs' identification of a *yagé* poetics, which affirms creative correspondence across decades between the visionary drug and cut-up methods, linked by reference to St.-Perse. Secondly, this identification draws attention to the specific stylistic parallels between St.-Perse's densely repetitive, image-rich, Whitmanesque catalogues, and Burroughs' *yagé*-inspired vision of the "Composite City," written earlier that July, which would conclude "In Search of Yage." In fact, there is a precise irony to the parallel Burroughs implies, since eight years earlier St.-Perse had actually made his own reference to the drug—remarkable, given how little it was known outside Amazonia—in his epic poem *Vents*. From one of Ginsberg's photographs taken in his Lower East Side apartment, we know that Burroughs read this just weeks later.[5] In which case, he would have come across the allusion to "*Yaghé, liane du pauvre, qui fait surgir l'envers des choses*" ("Yaghe, liana of the poor, that evokes the reverse of things"), and no doubt have been disappointed that St.-Perse was actually rejecting rather than embracing the visions fuelled by hallucinogenic drugs.[6]

---

5. See Ginsberg, *Photographs* (Altadena: Twelvetrees Press, 1990). The caption reads: "William Burroughs amusing himself with 1953's recent translation of St.-Jean Perse's *Vents*, living room floor 206 East 7th Street New York City, Fall '53" (n.pag.).

6. St.-John Perse, *Winds,* bilingual edition, translated by Hugh Chisholm (New York: Pantheon, 1953; 2nd edition, 1961), 128, 129. I am grateful to Professor Roger Little, the recognised authority on St.-Perse, for confirming this understanding: "his poetics is diametrically opposed to that induced by drug taking" (personal email, January 2006).

St.-Perse's other relevance here is thematic, and concerns the grand vision of human voyages and historical upheavals that informs the vatic style of his epic poems, *Anabase*—which Burroughs knew in T. S. Eliot's translation—and *Vents*, based on the poet's vision of America, where he had been living in exile since the war. There is a distinctly Spenglerian dimension to St.-Perse's sweeping reflections on the cyclical crises and regenerations of human destiny, on the relations between West and East, and on "the failure of past culture and the possibility of human annihilation."[7] Ginsberg's description that September of Burroughs' "Yage" manuscript—specifically, the "Composite City" vision—likewise recognised its affinity with "the anthropological-eastern deep psychic intensity of St. J-Perse's poetry." In the context of Burroughs' *Notebook,* swept by its own apocalyptic "winds of change and death" (43), the invocation of St.-Perse is emotionally darker, implicitly drawing together as it does his ill-fated individual voyage through the Americas and a larger vision of human history, one in which "The New World is a great lack, a yearning ache of despair" (79).

Burroughs' identifications with Kafka, Melville, Conrad, and St.-Perse add up to a more potent frame of reference than the trio of literary allusions in "In Search of Yage"—Truman Capote, Evelyn Waugh, and H. G. Wells, where only the latter's "The Country of the Blind" hits the theme of tragic Western destiny. The *Notebook,* however, makes clear that Burroughs' sense of looming cultural catastrophe is grounded in his own *private* crisis, culminating in a dramatic conclusion not about the future but about what has been and gone—and this judgement radically rewrites his journey through the Americas. Far from being about his desire to write or his quest to discover *yagé,* he sees the past seven months as a series of grievous personal losses that now haunt him like dreadful revenants: "I see the S.A. trip as a disaster that lost me everything I had of value. Bits of it keep floating back to me like memories of a day time nightmare" (77).

Informing his Latin American snapshots of disease and decay, and suggesting their projection of inner fears, this urgent experience of loss reaches its conclusion

---

7. Paul J. Archambault, "Westward the Human Spirit: Saint-John Perse's Vision of America," *Papers on Language and Literature* 23, no. 3 (Summer 1987): 379.

in the phrase Burroughs uses in one of the last entries to sum up his whole trip: "Everything lost" (97). These words precisely echo a moving report that Jack Kerouac had made in December 1952, when describing Burroughs' state as he departed Mexico City: "Burroughs is gone at last—3 years in Mexico—lost everything, his children, his patrimony [. . .]—all lost, dust, & thin tragic Bill hurries off into the night solitaire."[8] As the *Notebook* reveals, eight months later, back once again in Mexico City for a truly final departure, this bleak portrait was how Burroughs now saw himself.

"M"

Kerouac identified Burroughs' major personal losses, but their effect had been compounded over the following months by another absence and cause of solitude that appears in the *Notebook* as the elusive object of Burroughs' quest on his arrival in Mexico City: "I was looking only for one person. M" (19).

"M" was Lewis Marker, the reluctant lover Burroughs had taken with him on his first search for *yagé* in summer 1951, and who he fictionalised in 1952 as Allerton, William Lee's impossible object of desire in *Queer.* One of the major values of the *Notebook* is the support it gives to reassessing the importance of this relationship for his autobiographical fiction. Because it did not simply end in disaster in 1951, as *Queer* implies and as biographers and critics have assumed. To Burroughs, the relationship continued even in Marker's absence, with the paradoxical result—as the final section of this introduction will show—that it continued to have material consequences for his writing throughout 1952 and, as the *Notebook* reveals, 1953 as well.

Within the *Notebook* itself, Marker's phantom presence is absolutely central to the blurring of fact with fiction and to the slippages in space and time that characterise the Burroughsian world. Thus, immediately after describing his arrival in Mexico City to look for "M"—last seen there some ten months ago—Burroughs' compulsive quest segues into memories of another reality: "Like in a dream I had several times . . ." (19). This shift to noting his recurrent dream-searches happens so rapidly

---

that the "real" accounts of looking for Marker that follow take on themselves the quality of a repetitious dream. This impression is supported by the way in which Burroughs not only mixes his references to "M" or "Marker" with others to the fictional "Allerton," but seems to forget which is which, as when describing his experience of Mexico City as coloured by "an ache of memories of *Allerton*" (81; my italics). Open to the juxtaposition of travel notes, private reflections, fictional sketches, and dream reports, the hybrid and heterogeneous form of Burroughs' *Notebook* readily assimilates different kinds of materials and encourages their merger. For many writers, this confusion of fragments might have limited its usefulness; for Burroughs, this was precisely where he was going.

Under such conditions of ontological uncertainty, every detail comes to assume a "special significance" (31), an effect also of Burroughs' increasingly fragmentary, elliptical notations, which are all the more enigmatic for being often barely legible. Details acquire, in his definitive phrasing, the "cryptic significance of a dream" (37). This effect is surcharged by the disturbances in chronology produced by the form of the *Notebook* entries and the immediacy of the present tense in which they are written. As if acting out his recurrent dreams, events appear to be repeating themselves—compare pages 27 and 37, for example—and it takes a while to realise that Burroughs is in fact returning to a single event and redrafting his description. Likewise, by narrating in detail his journey to Mexico City (33–35) *after* he has already described arriving there (19), a curiously dreamlike temporality emerges, with flashes of déjà-vu and an uncanny sense of fateful circularity. The reading experience generated by this process of writing, by the form of the notebook itself, therefore seems to reproduce Burroughs' own experience of internal and external realities: "My mind goes round and round repeating" (77); "Nothing is happening completely by chance. There is the special significance to every meeting" (31); "Bits of it keep floating back to me like memories of a day time nightmare."

Burroughs' struggle to escape the traps of memory and desire may even account for the extraordinary sequence towards the end of the *Notebook* where the very words on the page give up their representational function and turn irreducibly cryptic. Here, the writing turns into a series of swirls and glyphs that might be mathematical symbols, characters from Hebrew or Greek or a version of Pitman shorthand (echoes of "In Search of Yage," perhaps, and his *yagé*-fuelled vision of "Hebephrenic shorthand"), before eventually forming itself into what looks like the drawing of a rose (85–93). Unique in Burroughs, the graphic, visceral aspect of these remarkable pages, and the accelerated and animate quality of his pencil strokes, does recall the products of other hallucinogen-driven artwork, especially that of Henri Michaux. His experiments with mescaline—first taken in 1954, and described in *Miserable Miracle*—resulted, as Michaux put it, in an "original text, more tangible than legible, drawn rather than written," where "letters ended in smoke or disappeared in zigzags."[9] It is possible that Burroughs had been taking *yagé*, since we know he had packed a quantity of the vine. Then again, it is also plausible to see these strange transformations of signs into symbols and symbols into drawings as a response to the knowledge, impelled by the narcotic ache of a compulsive desire, that it did not make things any better to write about them.

Although the *Notebook* has its own literary and aesthetic interest, and features some typically provocative ethnographic observations, it also offers a unique key to understanding the fluid state and surprising transformations of Burroughs' contemporaneous manuscripts. From the point of view of Burroughs scholarship, therefore, his relationship with Marker that haunts the *Notebook* is important because the writing here bridges in unexpected ways his manuscripts of "Queer" and "Yage." Paradoxically, to grasp this point we need to bear in mind the *absence* of Marker from Burroughs' writing since stopping work on "Queer" a year earlier. There are simply no references to him at all in any of Burroughs' surviving correspondence between January and July 1953, and of course he does not appear in "In Search of Yage," whose letters cover the same period. To look at this another way, the return of Marker/Allerton in the *Notebook*—or rather, Burroughs' return to memories and fantasies of him—would appear to link this material back to the unfinished "Queer" manuscript, and so separate it completely from "Yage." Appearances, however, prove highly deceptive, and at this point we need to explore in detail the *Notebook*'s richly complex and curious textual history in relation to Burroughs' other manuscripts.

---

9. Henri Michaux, *Miserable Miracle,* translated by Louise Varès (San Francisco: City Lights, 1963), 5.

Mexico City Return

The discontinuity signalled by Marker/Allerton's presence in the *Notebook* is all the more striking because it so flatly contradicts the expectations of any reader familiar with *The Yage Letters* who then opens the *Notebook*. For it begins chronologically and geographically (July 16, Talara, Peru) almost exactly where "In Search of Yage" left off (July 10, Lima, Peru). On closer inspection, what we find is not just continuity, however, but something much more paradoxical: verbatim overlap. For scattered among the first nine pages of the *Notebook* there is almost all the material that appears in "In Search of Yage" as the last page of the letter dated July 8 (which originally concluded the whole section, until the addition of the July 10 letter for the second edition of *The Yage Letters* in 1975). Comparing the two versions of this material, we recognise passages that in the *Notebook* describe Burroughs' journey *from* Lima (up to Talara) now used for the description of his earlier journey *to* Lima (from Pucallpa). But more is at stake here than the cannibalization of three hundred words, for the transposition of material from Burroughs' notebook into the form of a letter is in fact primary evidence of how he fabricated almost *all* the "letters" of "In Search of Yage."

In order to uncover the important part played by Burroughs' notebooks in the complex genesis of "In Search of Yage," we need to start from the fact that his "Yage" manuscript was effectively composed in three stages.[10] Firstly, he completed a 9,500 word typescript in early June 1953, which was epistolary in neither form nor origin, that became the first three-quarters of "In Search of Yage." He then produced additional material during June and July, about half of which was used to make the last quarter of "In Search of Yage." Finally, all this material was reworked in Ginsberg's New York apartment between September and early December, by which time it had acquired the formal appearance of letters. While it's not clear how much, if any, of the June manuscript originated in Burroughs' notes, it does possess a significant formal relation to the *Notebook;* Ginsberg's account to Malcolm Cowley accurately describes it as a "kind of self-invented journal form." In other words, before Burroughs created its epistolary appearance, the original manuscript of "Yage" was as close in form to the notebook as to the letter.

---

10. For a detailed account, see my Introduction to *The Yage Letters Redux* (San Francisco: City Lights, 2006), especially xxix–xxxv.

In the second stage of its manuscript history, the last quarter of what became "In Search of Yage," some 3,500 words, was assembled from Burroughs' notebook material and real letters (in a ratio of about two to one). It is likely that he kept just one notebook during this period, which has not survived. When he wrote Ginsberg in early July a letter that included "notes as they are in note-book, which is such a terrible mess I want to type the notes up and throw away the note-book" (*Letters* 173), it seems that this is exactly what he did. But because Burroughs retyped his notes into his letters to Ginsberg as new material to be added onto his "Yage" manuscript, much of the material from this lost notebook has been preserved. Three letters he wrote during early July together feature over three thousand words copied from that notebook (see *Letters* 169, 173–76, 178–80, 184–86), making it possible to compare his practice across notebooks. Equally, we can now see that Burroughs' real letter of July 8 was almost entirely made up of notes retyped from that notebook, and recognise there is no overlap at all with the letter of the same date that appears in "In Search of Yage."

In the third stage, Burroughs and Ginsberg—with the help of Alene Lee, who did the typing—reframed the materials by putting them into epistolary form. This created a loose overall unity by using the activity of letter writing to motivate an otherwise awkwardly discontinuous narrative made up of disparate fragments. Significantly, Burroughs would come up with a similar formal solution to similar structural problems exactly two years later in Tangier when working on what became *Naked Lunch*. Having used his regular letters to Ginsberg as a medium to record "miscellaneous ideas, a sort of running diary," in October 1955 he hit upon the idea "to alternate chapters of Letter and Journal Selections, with straight narrative chapters" (*Letters* 216, 288). After composing one "Letter and Journal" chapter of some forty pages, this arrangement was later abandoned, but traces of it remain in the published text in the form of sections entitled *"Disintoxication Notes," "Habit Notes,"* and *"Notes from yagé state,"* while Burroughs' Introduction would speak of the whole text as "notes which have now been published under the title *Naked Lunch*."[11] The formal presentation of all these "notes" clearly implies their origins in *notebooks*, although this is doubly misleading. Firstly, because it conceals the crucial genetic significance

---

11. *Naked Lunch: the restored text,* edited by James Grauerholz and Barry Miles (New York: Grove, 2003), 47, 55, 91, 199.

of letter-writing, the direct source for many of the novel's routines, and secondly because, while Burroughs probably did keep some notebooks during the writing of *Naked Lunch,* none appear to have survived. Whereas his closest friends, Ginsberg and Kerouac, always maintained notebooks, diaries, and journals—and have left behind dozens of examples for scholars to examine—throughout his first decade as a writer Burroughs did not.[12]

Finally, before moving on to explore the most extensive and significant relation between the *Notebook* and Burroughs' other manuscripts, there is one more, equally surprising, overlap with *The Yage Letters.* It is easily overlooked because it doesn't occur in "In Search of Yage," but in "I Am Dying, Meester?" the cut-up text from 1962 that completed the book. This text is clearly made by the recycling of fragments taken from "In Search of Yage"—nearly a quarter of its words come from the letters—mixed in with other materials composed much later. But almost a tenth derives from Burroughs' *Notebook,* including details such as his "rum coke" and the honky-tonk country song titles—"Your Cheating Heart" and "Driving Nails In My Coffin"—he hated so much.[13]

By far the most important—and indeed paradoxical—part in the textual history of the *Notebook* is its relation to *Queer,* more specifically its "Epilogue," "Mexico City Return." Comparing texts, the reader can recognise a third of "Mexico City Return"—some 850 out of 2,500 words—appears verbatim in the *Notebook,* scattered across its first twenty-four pages. In fact, the overlap seems much greater, since many parts, such as the account of Burroughs returning to Mexico City and looking for Allerton, have been simply expanded and lightly reworked. This material seems to continue where the main narrative of *Queer* leaves off: having departed Mexico City to travel through the jungles of Central America with Allerton, we now find Lee returning to Mexico City, apparently a week or two later. The upshot in terms of the chronology of Burroughs' biography, however, is the paradox of having to read "Mexico City Return"—based on material taken from the *Notebook* describing events

---

12. From the early 1960s, Burroughs did start to keep extensive scrapbooks that combined notes, images, and collages of material.

13. *The Yage Letters Redux,* 77.

in late summer 1953—as a seamless continuation of events that took place in late summer 1951, a full *two years* earlier.[14] Clearly, another understanding is necessary.

The immediate solution is to know that the "Epilogue" to *Queer* never belonged to Burroughs' "Queer" manuscript; it was added only during the process of editing in 1985, prompted by the publisher's request for more material to fill out the short and visibly incomplete original manuscript. Instead, "Mexico City Return" belonged to Burroughs' "Yage" manuscript.[15] Indeed, this was one of the major unused parts composed in the second stage of the manuscript's history, during July and August 1953. This knowledge clears up the puzzle of chronology, however, only to produce other, even more puzzling consequences. For if the material taken from the first two dozen pages of Burroughs' *Notebook* and later published as "Mexico City Return" was once a part of "In Search of Yage," then Allerton must have been a part of it too—which he was. Equally, if this material appeared in the manuscript of "In Search of Yage," then it must have been recast in epistolary form—which it was.[16]

In short, the *Notebook* makes apparent the remarkable fluidity of Burroughs' manuscripts, both in content and form, complicating our assumptions about the identities of the texts both as written and as published. What's striking is the sheer contingency of the three manuscripts that Burroughs wrote during his Mexican years—"Junk," "Queer," and "Yage"—whose now-familiar forms were actually shaped by a chain of circumstance and necessity tied to the economic logic of publication: because his editors at Ace wanted to expand the brief Mexican ending of "Junk," in 1952 Burroughs cannibalized the opening chapters of "Queer," and because what was left of that manuscript was so short as well as incomplete, when Viking came

---

14. This chronological slippage is evident in Lee's anxiety on arriving at Mexico City airport; nothing in *Queer* explains his sudden fear of the police, because its basis—Burroughs' legal status in Mexico after shooting his wife—relates to events after its narrative ends.

15. The provenance of the material explains the otherwise unaccountable shift in narrative point of view in *Queer,* as the third person gives way in the "Epilogue" to the first.

16. Most of this material probably featured in a fabricated letter, "July 20, Mexico City," while the accounts of first-hand witnesses such as Robert Creeley and Alan Ansen confirm that it was part of the "Yage" manuscript in 1955; see Ansen's essay, "Anyone Who Can Pick Up a Frying Pan Owns Death," first published in *Big Table* no. 2 (1959), reprinted in *The Burroughs File* (San Francisco: City Lights, 1984). Stanford holds a copy of the last six pages of the August typescript, repaginated 39–44, indicating their location within a version of the "Yage" manuscript (Ginsberg Papers, Correspondence Series 1, Box 2, Folder 42, Stanford University).

to publish it thirty years later *Queer* gained a convenient "Epilogue"—which would have already been included in *The Yage Letters* in 1963, had that volume not collected together only those sections of "Yage" already printed in magazines. It's possible to imagine completely different combinations of this early material, and in Mexico City during late summer 1953—a time curiously forgotten in all the standard biographies—Burroughs sat down with his notebook and did precisely that.

"No Word from Allerton"

The potential for alternative versions of what became "In Search of Yage" and *Queer* is contemplated in one of Burroughs' final entries in the *Notebook*. Here, in a series of seemingly cryptic notes, he plots out an entirely different future for his material (97):

> When Lee quit junk—unexpurgated version—First trip to S.A. with Allerton. Return to Mexico. Left out—Allerton goes and returns—Back to S.A. No word from Allerton, S.A. trip and back to Mexico. Everything lost—

Decoding these notations, Burroughs here envisages creating a single text out of six elements. First is the "unexpurgated version" of when Lee quit junk, by which he actually means the original beginning of "Queer." For in August 1952 Burroughs had stripped the first two chapters of his "Queer" manuscript to form a 5,500-word insert for the last, Mexican-set, quarter of "Junk" (105–19 in *Junky*)—and he now envisages restoring all the material he had edited out, which included Lee's first encounter with Allerton.[17] The second element— "First trip to S.A. with Allerton"—would correspond to the last chapters of "Queer" (79–121 in *Queer*). The third part—"Return to Mexico"—can only refer to Burroughs' return journey, alone, from Ecuador in September 1951. This might then explain the phrase, "Left out"—which itself leaves out its apparently unspeakable referent; namely Burroughs' shooting, that September,

---

17. See my Introduction and the endnotes in *Junky: the definitive text of "Junk"* (New York: Penguin, 2003), xxvi–xxvii and 163–64.

of Joan. No manuscript exists for this episode, nor for the next—"Allerton goes and returns"—although Burroughs' biography determines that it covers the period from January to September 1952. The fifth section—"Back to S.A."—refers to the travels Burroughs began in January 1953, followed by "S.A. trip and back to Mexico," which would cover the sixth months to July as described in "In Search of Yage" plus the *Notebook* entries that became "Mexico City Return." The final phrase—"Everything Lost"—therefore glosses a narrative that combines both Burroughs' 1951 and 1953 *yagé* trips, that is framed by two sets of departures from and to Mexico City, and that is centred around the search for, and loss of, Allerton.[18] Had events worked out differently, this composite manuscript would have been Burroughs' sequel to *Junkie*.

Allerton's paradoxically negative presence supplies still further links between Burroughs' manuscripts that point towards not only alternative possibilities, but new understandings of the texts as published. First, however, we need to take one stage further the already long and complex textual history of "Mexico City Return." The material that had started out as entries in Burroughs' *Notebook*, that later featured in the epistolary "Yage" manuscript, and that was eventually published as an epilogue to the narrative of *Queer* also existed in another form. For the "Mexico City Return" section was not based directly on the *Notebook* fragments, but upon a ten-page typescript that Burroughs composed at the very beginning of August (and mailed on the 3rd to Ginsberg as an addition to "Yage").[19] This August manuscript was mainly an expansion of the *Notebook* material (only two out of its ten pages have no direct relation) and, at 3,800 words long, was fifty percent longer than "Mexico City Return." About a third of the August manuscript, therefore, was not used in the Epilogue to *Queer*. There was also more material originally from the *Notebook* in the manuscript, so that, altogether, a full quarter of the *Notebook* was used to make it. Having already culled several thousand words from his first notebook during early July, Burroughs clearly started his second with a definite idea of its potential literary use.

---

18. In 1955 Burroughs wrote a "new introduction" to his "Yage" manuscript set in Mexico that seems to have projected a very similar circularity for his 1953 trip by creating the "continuity of journey from Mexico to S.A. and back to Mexico" (*Letters* 251, 253).

19. Ten-page untitled typed manuscript (Ginsberg Collection, Columbia University).

Among the material present in the August manuscript that was not used for "Mexico City Return" is a doubly significant opening frame: "Back in Lima. No letter from Allerton. I felt sick and discouraged and sat down for several minutes in the embassy. Why doesn't he write?" This emphatic new beginning takes up epistolary references scattered throughout the *Notebook:* the repeated line, "So he got all my letters. Why didn't he answer. Why?" (25, 43)—which was present in the August manuscript, but again edited out of "Mexico City Return" for *Queer;* and the phrase "No Word from Allerton" in Burroughs' alternative plan for his manuscripts. Here, "No Word" means "no letters," as is clear from the covering note he sent Ginsberg with his August manuscript: "I didn't mention it before because I did not feel like talking about it, that I never heard from Marker after I left Mexico, though I wrote ten letters to his home address in Florida to be forwarded" (*Letters* 187). These references to the broken epistolary relation between Burroughs and Marker are highly significant because his letter writing had covertly structured the writing of his "Queer" manuscript during 1952. When he stopped work on it that October, Burroughs would tell Ginsberg that he "wrote *Queer* for Marker" (*Letters* 138), but he had also generated key parts of it—at least some of Lee's routines—by writing *to* him.[20]

What the *Notebook* and the August manuscript derived from it establish is that Burroughs planned to incorporate this epistolary structure, with its creative as well as emotional economy, into his writing. And what's more, this plan predated the decision to recast his "Yage" manuscript into epistolary form. This final point makes visible a particular irony in the most compelling piece of evidence for the intended continuity of Burroughs' material. For, immediately after the opening frame, with its despair at failing to receive letters, the August manuscript continues with all the material taken from his *Notebook* that, just a few weeks later, would become the last page of the July 8 letter in "In Search of Yage."

The second significance of the August manuscript's opening frame is its unexpected and striking echo of another passage: "I stopped off at the U.S. Embassy [. . .]

---

20. See my *William Burroughs and the Secret of Fascination* (Carbondale: Southern Illinois University Press, 2003), 133–57.

No letters." Here, the embassy in question is not Lima in July 1953 but Panama in January, and these phrases occur in the very first letter of "In Search of Yage" (4).[21] Although he goes unnamed, and the reference is easily missed, a ghostly trace of Allerton does therefore appear in *The Yage Letters* after all, and takes the most appropriate possible form: a cryptic allusion to his epistolary absence.[22]

Finally, the *Notebook* and the August manuscript shed new light on the writing and significance of one of Burroughs' most potent and enigmatic routines, which at one stage might have completed his "Yage" manuscript and would later form the ending to *Queer*—the sinister story of Friendly Finance. First drafts of this material appear early on in the *Notebook* (11–13), without any apparent context. In the August manuscript, Burroughs now introduced it with the line, "Thought up gag for if I find Allerton"—at a later point, he amended the word "gag" to "routine"[23]—and by the time it was edited for *Queer* thirty years later it had changed again, to, "That night I dreamed I finally found Allerton" (132). In the *Notebook,* neither the situation nor the identities of the routine's speaker and audience are clear, since it is initially addressed, most curiously, to "Bill," and then to "Louie" (11)—a sign, perhaps, that the more developed narrative context would actually dramatize a disguised truth. This possibility is hinted at in an entry made two weeks later (August 1–3), when Burroughs develops the routine in order to reflect on the "degree of reciprocity" in his "contract" with Marker. His conclusion—that real contact with another is impossible, that what "you want to contact" is "in fact part of *yourself*" (61)—lays bare the intra-psychic dimension to what had seemed an interpersonal relationship. In other words, Burroughs was addressing himself, playing both roles in the routine, both the one who will never let go and the one desperate to escape.

What the *Notebook* and the August manuscript also reveal is that Burroughs wrote the material in two stages, since there is a gap between the appearance of the representative of Friendly Finance and—"three days later," according to an aside

---

21. This passage did not appear in Burroughs' original June "Yage" manuscript, but was added during Fall 1953, very probably after he had decided on an epistolary structure.

22. At one point in the manuscript history, "In Search of Yage" actually included a letter from Lee to Allerton; see *The Yage Letters Redux,* xxxvii and 86–87.

23. Ginsberg Papers, Correspondence Series 1, Box 2, Folder 42, Stanford University.

on the manuscript—his metamorphosis into the Skip Tracer. There is a portent of this creepy, fantomatic figure, clearly a creature from the dream dimension, in the first sketch—"It hurts our feelings when a client skips out on us" (11)—but the *Notebook* does not contain a draft of this second half. Instead, following on from a broken line at the foot of the page—"But Friendly Finance never" (59)—and preceding the discussion of the "contract," there appears a tantalising blank space marked by the stubs of four sheets torn from the book. Did Burroughs first sketch the Skip Tracer on those pages, and possibly reveal more about his nightmarish self-portrait as a psychic repo man? Perhaps the absence of these four pages, this hole at the heart of Burroughs' *Notebook,* can be taken to materialise his desolate sense of all that is lost, irredeemably lost, in life and therefore in our own quest to repossess the secrets of the past.

comments on the text

BY GEOFFREY D. SMITH

It is an unassuming school notebook in plain, black paper wrappers—a type sold in Mexico and Latin America in the 1950s—somewhat square in shape, eight by six inches, with cheap lined paper, forty-eight leaves in all with the stubs of four missing leaves following leaf twenty-nine. And it traveled through much of Latin America, from Peru to Mexico, in the hands of William S. Burroughs who, with a number two lead pencil, crafted events, emotions, inchoate plots and themes in addition to doodling and scribbling. This unique literary document is part of the larger William S. Burroughs Collection in the Rare Books and Manuscripts Library at The Ohio State University Libraries. That *The Latin American Notebook of William S. Burroughs* survived the years (see Oliver Harris' "Introduction" to this volume regarding the textual history) and arrived at Ohio State can only be attributed to good fortune.

The *Notebook* went to auction as lot 22 of the *Allen Ginsberg and Friends* sale held at Sotheby's New York on October 7, 1999. The Rare Books and Manuscripts Library of The Ohio State University Libraries was bidding by telephone. In the fury of the bidding, Ohio State had already exceeded its allocated funds and made one final bid that held. Had the competitors but made the minimal raise, the *Notebook* would have been destined elsewhere. As it turned out, the *Notebook* was united with other significant Burroughs materials at Ohio State including about a third of the original *Naked Lunch* typescript, other various early manuscripts and correspondence, and virtually the entire literary archive of the Burroughs' corpus from 1972 until his death in 1997. Among significant, discrete manuscript archives, for instance, are the multiple drafts of his trilogy *Cities of the Red Night* (1981), *The Place of Dead Roads* (1983), and *The Western Lands* (1987).

As a nascent document in the Burroughs' corpus, it seemed critical for Burroughs research that this text become accessible to the international scholarly community. The general editors of the project, Geoffrey D. Smith and John M. Bennett, approached The Ohio State University Press with regard to publishing the *Notebook*. Not only did the press see the value of such a publication but expressed a desire to publish other Burroughs works. With the cooperation of James Grauerholz, literary executor of the Burroughs estate, and the outstanding contributions of Oliver Harris, Burroughs scholar and volume editor, this book is the first volume of a Burroughs collection that will include a forthcoming, newly edited version of *The Revised Boy Scout Manual.*

Titled *Everything Lost: The Latin American Notebook of William S. Burroughs,* the volume in hand includes: a digital facsimile reproduction of the *Notebook*; an edited fair text version; and a documentary transcription of all the text of the *Notebook,* including excisions. Each of these textual versions serves a specific purpose. The facsimile, from a high-resolution digital scan, does, of course, afford the audience a highly accurate view of the text as artifact. The facsimile provides a feel, a flavor, for the writer at work where one can observe Burroughs' hand as it alters according to mood or moment. The deletions (casual at some points and vigorous at others), the erasures, the re-workings, the inserts—all attest to Burroughs' crafting of the text. And, finally, the reader can witness, and, perhaps sympathize with, the editorial task of deciphering Burroughs' challenging penmanship. As noted in editorial notes, in some cases the editors openly admit that a chosen word or phrase is, quite simply, a best guess. With the facsimile available to all, the reader can judge personally as to the quality of editorial choice, and, of course, proffer alternative readings. The editorial goal has always been to identify each exact word of the *Notebook* in order to render, as nearly as possible, an unmediated text. That a wholly unmediated text cannot be provided will be evident when the facsimile *Notebook* is read: some words, to the current editors, at least, are simply indecipherable from internal examination. The few indecipherable portions are indicated by †, a symbol that Burroughs does not use elsewhere in the *Notebook*. Some editorial judgments are augmented by context or external evidence, such as other works by Burroughs, and are documented in the notes to the text.

The importance of the complete transcription, then, is to capture the mind at work and observe subtexts to what is earlier presented as the fair copy. The question of authorial intention is not at play in this documentary edition of the *Notebook*, because there is only one state of the text. Therefore, whatever Burroughs crossed out still appears in the complete transcription, but is deleted from the fair copy. With both versions at hand, however, in addition to the digital facsimile, readers can draw their own conclusions regarding editorial decisions. For instance, as Oliver Harris notes in the "Introduction," Burroughs quotes from Mahler's *Das Lied von der Erde.* The Mahler citation is crossed out in the *Notebook,* albeit less rigorously than other excisions, but still clearly deleted. The editorial decision, then, was to exclude this substantive passage from the fair copy, as tempting as it was for the editors to include it. Still, its inclusion in the transcription admits it to *a* text, if not *the* text that the editors designate as the fair copy. That is to say, there are no editorial claims to the fair copy being a definitive edition, but rather, the three textual presentations—facsimile, fair copy, and transcription—provide the framework for a scholarly edition. The facsimile provides the original document in Burroughs' hand; the fair copy presents a text selected from the non-excised portions of the *Notebook,* presumably a text crafted by the author; and the transcription presents a literal rendition of the facsimile, with no word or punctuation being unaccounted for (though others may read any word differently).

Burroughs typically wrote on only one side, the recto, of a notebook leaf. Still, there are ample instances of writing on the verso. In almost all cases, these verso recordings appear to have been added separately from the recto writings. Also, it appears that the verso writings most generally have a narrative, imaginative or logical relation to text on the facing page (i.e., the recto of the following leaf), rather than the reverse of the current leaf. Hence, in layout, when there is text on the verso, it is displayed with text from the facing page as related, creative units. The sole exception is the verso of leaf twenty-nine (page 60), which would have faced the recto of the first of four leaves cut from the *Notebook.* It cannot be determined if that section, the verso of leaf twenty-nine, referred to an earlier, discarded text, or the resumed text, which continues the "Friendly Finance" routine from the recto of leaf twenty-nine. Also, more typical than not, when Burroughs was recording on the recto he would add inserts on those very leaves, lending further credence to the belief that the recordings on the verso leaves were added later.

Textual notes are incorporated in the transcription text. Though reluctant to be gratuitous in most cases of identification of people, settings or events, the editors did not want to err with too little elucidation. For instance, the reference to Ethel and Julius Rosenberg (p. 141 [facsimile p. 61]) will be obvious to any scholar of mid-twentieth century American cultural history, but it seemed appropriate to emphasize that their execution occurred but a month before the inception of the *Notebook.* In the cases of grammar and idiosyncratic spellings, the editors chose to record text as Burroughs wrote it. For instance, on page 137 [facsimile p. 51], the editors retained Burroughs' spelling of *inocense,* which is repeated elsewhere in the *Notebook.* In some cases, Burroughs spells the same word differently, even on the same page: thus, on page 144 [facsimile p. 73], he writes *gentleness,* but further down he writes *gentelness*; on page 143 [facsimile p. 67], he writes *immigrant,* but shortly after he writes *imigrants.* The editors also retained Burroughs' individual use of contractions and accents, thus, *Dont* for Don't on page 135, [facsimile p. 45], and *vamonos* for vámonos on page 132 [facsimile p. 35]. In instances where Burroughs was being consciously playful with language, e.g., dialogue or the "riff" of the complete page 149 [facsimile p. 95], there are no notes. **Bolded** terms and phrases in the notes indicate that they appear as recorded from the text. The decision to attach all notes to the transcription text was, precisely, to leave the fair text free of overt editorial intervention and commentary.

Variant readings are also noted in the transcription. These are cases where there was no editorial consensus regarding specific words with decisions being determined by context, grammar, spelling idiosyncracies of Burroughs, cursive style, etc.

Since this is the first publication of *Everything Lost,* derived from a holograph manuscript, there is no additional authorial intervention. Certainly, as amply demonstrated in the "Introduction," specific language and themes recur through Burroughs' later works (whole sections in some cases), and those works have been useful in determining difficult passages. But, this volume remains essentially a documentary text. The facsimile is a digital reproduction of the actual notebook; the fair copy is our edited version of the transcription; and the transcription is, as nearly as possible, an exact recording of this unique text. For a line-by-line transcription of the holographic original, readers and scholars can refer to the original 2008 edition of this work.

notebook

Talara.   July 14.
A bus called Proletaria just
passed the bar where I am
drinking my 5. P.M. pisco. [Got to
watch drinking I can black out on
4 drinks now.]
Trip up from Lima not too bad,
as I shoved off with a tube of
codeinetas and two nembies, and
floated 12 hours. Rather a nice
batch of Ecuadorians and Bolivians
returning from Buenos Aires. Three
times "all the foreigners" had to
get out and register with the police.
What do they do with these records.
use them as toilet paper I expect.
Talara is in a desert that runs
right down to the sea. Nothing
grows here except a few wretched
palms around Company Houses.
This is a company town. Oil
refinery.] Saw a terrible Spanish
film. A woman representing death
would appear now and then in a

most J. The audience laughed all through the film. Young kids mostly. Some incredible items on the hotel menus. "Lobsters cooked in whiskey." "Scrambled children in piquant sauce." This is a misprint. I think they meant niños not niños

Last few days in Lima: cold and damp. The mercado Mayorista seems to have gone more or less sour. Saw a mi t Proportioned. He looked years older. Last time I saw him he wasn't drinking. Now he drinks all the time. Knife scar under the left eye. Feel that everybody has gone somewhere else. The place isn't the same.

Tried to sell what I didn't want to lot to the landlord. He gave me a low price on a few items, contracted to buy the rest the day I left at 9. A.M. By 3:30 he still hadn't showed. Figuring the gringo would leave that stuff for nothing, I gave most of it to an ice cream vendor.

Some to a good toothed Chinese waiter, who was suspicious of the deal and did not thank me. Some people can't believe anyone is giving them anything.

July 17, Panama.
© Rains of 1910. Limed trees— Wooden hospitals where people died in rows from yellow fever. Walked around with camera. People always know when you are taking their picture. Concept of soul loss. ~~through pictures~~. I was trying to get picture of young Indian on boat. Such languid animal innocence. He knew I was trying to take his picture and would always look up just as I was swinging camera into position. (Corrugated iron roofs, ~~~~ walking abatoires. Every old crofers like junk sickness, what do I want from him? sitting leaning against the

8

bow of the boat idly scratching
one shoulder — a long white scar
on his right shoulder — looking
up at me with a trace of ~~sullenness~~
sullenness. Walked around, started
cooking. Kept to me Angelo
again.

Photography. There is something obscene
here, ~~the~~ desire to capture, imprison the
incorporate.

Whis persistent pimps in Panama.
One stopped me chewing my ear
off about a 15 year old girl. I
told him. "She's middle aged
already, I want that 6 year old
ass. Don't try palming your
old 14 year old butt off on
me."

Everyone here is telepathic on
paranoid level. If you look at
anyone he knows at once he
is being observed and gives
evidence of hostility and
suspicion and sulenness.

[I represent the Friendly, Famous Co. Haven't you forgotten something, Bill. Don't mind if I call you Bill do you? We like to keep on familiar terms with our clients. You've been a bad boy. ~~You knew~~ You're supposed to come and see us every third Tuesday. We've been lonely for you in the office. ~~It hurts our feelings to have a client~~ ~~skip out on us.~~ We're friendly folk, Louie, and we don't like to ~~pay~~ pay up or else. I wonder if you ever read the contract; all of it. I have particular reference to clause 6 x which can only be deciphered with an electric microscope and a benus filter. I wonder if you know just what ~~the~~ the means, Louie.

Ah I know how it is with you young kids. Careless, workmanship irresponsible, They always give me the young ones because I know how to handle young kids: They all see the bigger and fancy

no matter how you slice it.

It's not a friendly thing to do.

up, after a little heart to
heart talk with ~~good~~ old
uncle Willy] ~~your side~~ ~~remember to~~
~~write to~~

On I know how it is with you anyway.
~~while~~ You get to ~~throw~~ after the
~~flower~~ a forget about ~~war~~ ~~the~~
T ~~Trung Trung~~ ~~it that~~, don't
you? But I ~~am~~ I ~~can~~ ~~the~~ don't
forget you. ~~I tell you anything I say~~
~~to know from one to~~
~~as a son say~~ ~~to think I be.~~
~~do be~~. But well why ~~you~~ ~~want~~
~~on a job~~. The older guy ~~me~~ the
young ones, because I know how
to ~~talk~~ handle you kid.

The inhabitants. A smog of beer fumes hangs over the town in the wet heat. ~~I am a picket demanding jobs for Paraguaian no men~~ The place ~~test~~ has changed since I left, ~~too~~ everything but that awful hillbilly music on the juke boxes — like the bellowing of a discontented cow, and the service men all look bovine and oddly blunted or brutalized as if they had received some special processing to fit them for peace time army life in a tight occupation. You ask them a question and they answer it, and that is that. Conversation is impossible. They have nothing to say. They sit around buying drinks for the B girls like the stupid young yokels they are, and making mechanical passes without any real passion, just something to

do, and playing that awful music. How could anyone be stupid enough to enjoy that bleating, whining crap. "It wasn't God Made Honky Tonk," and "You're driving Nails in My Coffin" and "Your Cheatin' Heart" — last days in Lima. Nobody around the bar in the Mercado Mayorista. Nothing brings you down like you go in a place you used to like and ~~nobody~~ there is nobody you know and everything is changed. The bar is in a different place, the juke box ~~moved~~, different waiters so you can't be sure you are in the same place. I suddenly decided to leave Lima at once, as if I ~~was~~ ~~first with this down in~~ had an urgent appointment somewhere else. This feeling of urgency has grown in me ever ~~t~~ the S.A. I have to be somewhere

at a certain time. It seems
vitally important to get the
1.30 P.M. plane and not
wait over until 11 A.M. the
next day. In Guayaquil I
went to the house of the Peruvian
consul after his office hours
so I could get a visa and
leave one day early. Where
am I going? Appointment in
Talara & Tingo Maria, Pucallpa,
Panama, Guatemala, Mexico —
I don't know. Suddenly I have
to leave right now.

[B'nai in Chico's. Her shallow
bird mind. Perfect English like a
recording.

                    Mexico City.

was checked in Hotel and went
straight to Tato's. No use asking
Pepe for info. He wouldn't know
where anybody was. I was looking
only for one person. M. Like
in a dream I had several times

are draw told me by own
and admitted I was a unique
character."

I was back in Mexico, talking to
Eddie and or Louis Cargis.
Then came the pause and we
both drum on the tables while
worrying what I am going to
say. next "Where is M?" Dream about
M so many times. Usually we
are on good terms but
sometimes he is nasty and I keep
asking why and never find out.
Thursday going up to N.Y. to
Enlist I in Ambulance corps.
Louie told me she is in Aguas-
diente. South somewhere; [as I
ask when the bus leaves] only
one with dream and I can't recall
the details.] L. Cargis always there.
First dream in back seat of
car. incredibly nasty. Later
recognized such dry road. Talk
are I going north, I'm singing
"Walking my Baby Back Home." Hotel
Central and M.

Mitchell

was in Peru? Question of
going back for more George.
Roads impassable for restaurant.
Beggars with withered hand —
† [Tajachula] Young U.S. offered
him 10 c and would not take
it. Another beggar selling
Colombian lottery tickets. Young
man with odd shirt [blue &
[yangles] U.S. St Louis docks
yard. Saw him there in a bar.
Ayereise to M. [He was in gangster
hole out at & went to find him]
Beggar info on M. Mitchell — Brave
career. The H. chose character. A
woman. Going back to Tajachula
— Pucallpan.
Railway overrun with beggars and
lots of foreigners back there now.
When it & run old around then we
Colombian lottery tickets. No good
here. He wanted a part ow
puzzled. He never thought of that
like M looks sometimes when I
men on the point of committing friendship.

Sometimes I feel sorry for Albertson
He is such a child in a
way, and he sulks, and
callous and sulky, and sweet.
But he doesn't realize
what he is involved in. Yet
at times I feel for my own
further, as if it was some sort
creation of violent, unyielding
forces. Sometimes he looks
tired and puzzled, by the
worried intensity of my
emotions. He wants help
friendship, not a relationship
balancing on anxiety.
as no more suitable for the
fuel. Anyone born than I am
limited to endure the fear
or pain and misery.

First in Totos shook hands with
Pops — Talked the old retired
regular army man. Asked about
M. last. "By the way _____"
He didn't know M. Started
walking around at random.
Went into Store and looked at the
magazines. Pictures of a skywriter
in one there. If any really books or
things had on my Shoulder. yak.
Ran through the lot. All gone.
M.? I saw him about a month
ago on the other side of the
Street. ~~Talk it~~ It was like a
man his short of desolation,
a cold spending misere the
walk in ice boys, and around
the heart. I leaned against the
magazine rack. "I'll in you
see." I walked out and done
against a post. So he got all
my letters. Why didn't he come
by? I walked down to 154.
Looked in not a familiar face

The pain which stays and hurts
as a physical wound. I walked
back to Sears. Passed Zak
and nodded. Burdo to Tator.
Talked to Mitchell. Eddie knows,
Cross, so did Gore. Is at you
hear about M? No I said. He
went down to S. A or some place
with a colonel or a general. "So."
"How long ago did he leave?"
About six months ago. I could
feel the pain ease up a bit.
"Must have been right after I
left. "Yeah just about then".
I got Carpus address, and
went over to see him. Met
him as I was leaving the
hotel. Yes M. left about 5
months ago and went along
as guide to a major and his
wife. They were going to sell
the car in Tunisia. 647
miles. I felt there was something
a little wrong about the deal.

I could feel the pain surface up on one or I listened. To what would he be doing and where? Guatemala is expensive. Just what was the deal. San Salvador ever appearance on just water. Costa Rica? Perhaps. I regretted not having visited San José on way up. "It's me wonder what young you doing there? Evidently he had no complaint against me. I felt better after talking to Irene.

Where is everybody? Eddie on Cross and John one in Calif. & Run or John in Alaska. Like talking to Farmer or some one like killing the times again. Awa— where is anyway. So on So went wrong. So be is on just. So on as dead from any Brandon J. oh he's ill so so he's always around. The your father of Spee. True have around somehow, the even word of

Change and death and the
Chance meeting. Mitchell with
the missing fingers, old Phil,
the friend himself damaged
deaths life and change, and
the affairs significance. ~~by chance~~
~~meeting~~. nothing is happening
completely by chance. There is
the special significance to every
meeting.

Today for M.

I got out of the plane and waited
for the tourist. to ~~collect for~~
~~but a wide stare that~~
~~began gesture.. on his~~
~~hand bag and his camera.~~
"Lets take a car into town. Spent
it. Changes that money". We
walked through the airport like
father and son. I took off my
glasses and my hat was pushed
away in a suitcase. I had my
camera slung over my shoulder.
Two tourists.
"yes" I am ~~saying~~ "that old
boy in ~~Mukinales~~ wanted to
change 2.00 ~~$~~ from the
Palace Hotel out to the airport.
I told him 8]. "I held up a finger"
~~~~ no one
looked at us. ~~He off~~ ~~cab driver~~
We got in a taxi. The driver said
12 for town.
"Wait a minute" the I told him.

"No meter. Where is your meter.
You got to have a meter."
The driver asked me to explain
they were authorized to carry
air line passengers without
meter.
"No" she shouted. "Go on take me
to the Regis. But I pay what
is on the meter, Pedro. I call
it Pedro. You're required to
have a meter."
oh well I thought. That's all I
need, this cold jerk
should call the law. He was
yelling out of the car and taking
down the number. "I need police
plenty quick" he said.
I said "well I think I'll kick this
car anyway". "bananas" I said to
the driver. We started on through
the outskirts of Mexico, boys
playing baseball, trees in
open lots and I went to
come this way every morning to

37

...

anything. I sat down with an
adjacent punch. ~~The~~ The
old Major walked in.
Retired Regular army "grey haired
vigorous, short. With him a
young man I had seen before
with another retired army
man. ~~Heavy ahead,~~ full
lips, ~~a bulbous nose the most~~
~~ugly this way.~~
Dark, strong brows, full red lips,
handsome, ~~trading with~~ ~~nor on~~
~~trading after the year, perverse~~
I saw him walking around
with bags carrying bundles, I
figured the old Captain was
picking up the checks. A ~~spendthrift~~
Mormon, speculating in Alaska
~~amor now with~~ Russians. Lower, of
poor fire ~~here~~ with a silly grin,
I ran through the last employee
with the Major. And last of
all "what happened to M?" "I
don't think I know him."

oh "nice see you." I dropped the
Interviews on the table and walked
out. Sears magazine counter.
"Sorry Yon— Yes. Retired army.
All gone. I never see those guys
anyway. Never have worked on
T otei's any more—" "M?" "He's gone
too." "How long ago?" — No need
to be careful. He won't matter
anything. "I saw him about a
month ago on the other side of
the street." ~~I I felt like a moving~~
~~him shot it. I could afterday~~
A cold wave of misery and pain
~~settled~~ his in him a man here
what, ~~and~~ settling in the days are
around the heart. Then I knew
it was him again M. just the
same as ever. I put the magazine
away slowly, and walked outside
and leaned against a post. ~~When~~
~~like passing the train, everybody~~
~~put gone away and left me~~

Claim shown - Not very
on new surface, not larger
shadow theme

~~Like I~~ I was ~~suggesting~~ from m
~~ly~~ time gap. ~~Left completely alone~~
~~in a crowd in places where~~
~~I felt like~~ ~~I don't~~ I missed the
last train out of the Penal
Colony. Everybody else ~~on the~~ ~~of the~~
~~boat~~ gone. A chill of final
desolation and ~~separation~~. He ~~may have not~~ got the
letters why didn't he answer why?
~~Something to the most~~
~~important~~

§ The world of ~~Chess a one-to-one space~~
~~with very ~~
Across roads of Space-Time travel ^
~~worlds of change~~ and
death, dispersion — A waiting
room — when you queue a queue's divis.
dupe to your train leaves.
And fear of being left alone
in the waiting room after all
the trains had left.
Codi's word for Los Angeles —
? Rum and gin of Alaska
and Houston. Billy gone for
tuscaroon. John of the Plum.

Marker for. There's my train
Where to? I can't tell you
Where to? ~~[illegible]~~
~~[illegible]~~
The answer suggested by distance.
I can't catch the marker. Should
I turn in my ticket? It will be
one you'll never find here.
~~[illegible]~~
~~[illegible]~~ You'll end
up in a waiting room ~~[illegible]~~
~~[illegible]~~ where
the train doesn't stop anymore,
the tracks grown over with weeds,
~~[illegible]~~
~~[illegible]~~ jangle ~~[illegible]~~ clinkers
and the station master with doubled
legs, listening to the whistle
of M's train fading in the
distance, across the dead
yards, and red brick towns of
~~[illegible] 191~~8. of [illegible]
1918. [The station master is
[illegible] my [illegible] battle by anyone].

Jangle battle by [illegible] and the [illegible]

~~instead to~~ ~~and~~ the ~~morning~~ ~~paper~~
~~the~~ ~~form~~ ~~he~~ ~~now~~ ~~at~~ ~~the~~
~~the is for,~~

"You're movie" What is on my
ticket. I can't read it. Screwing
his ~~eyes up close~~ into Shall I turn it on?
~~Better~~ Wait for your own train.
on yellow paper.

~~For Casper and Pepi, are~~ ~~still~~
~~For_____~~

[For Casey or Pepi ain't words
for Casey. They are in the ground]
That is why you can stand to
live in Mexico City or N.Y. because
you are not stuck there. You
can dig the ~~past~~ of ~~the~~ ~~live~~ —
~~you~~ ~~try~~ ~~wonder of the~~ thinking
in Panama. ~~The~~ ~~as~~ ~~each~~ i
can smell of the world. ~~Taking~~
~~is no~~ feel of ~~travel~~ You
are you ultimately merely there,
~~take~~ spirit ~~Bought~~ in
~~trying~~ ~~crying~~ arguing ~~to~~ ~~travel~~
~~travel~~ Alike and trouble. And you
have to Mark the ~~arguments~~ ~~arts~~
PAN ~~and~~ ~~on~~ 4 h D all
live for removal of the body.

The football

The edges of the field, always
for them for a moment
they long lines of purple.
to end the day
As dejeuner ensues or
end. They are just proficient

Otherwise it would stay there —
not in the muggy heat under
a galvanized tin roof not
[illegible] a [strikethrough] [illegible] down slow
Cliff over the [illegible] bay where
vultures sat fish entrails not done
[strikethrough] trade. You can't wait
for you [strikethrough] out
of there. You then drove
ship in Panama. [strikethrough]
In Lima only now an then
and better not miss it. In
Guatemala City maybe once
in [illegible] get. In Bogotá
you can [illegible] get a [illegible]
to you [illegible] on a Point 4 car.
Ecuador has no service.
Not [illegible] — Ruis & Johnny.
Ruth and June — Eddie in L.A.
the [strikethrough] of [strikethrough]
last stop for C.S. P.P.S
trouble with the hoodlum
con man and the young wife.
Bill's water blue eyes [strikethrough]
[illegible] N.Y. [illegible]

unconditional

~~their blows~~
waiting for the N.Y. Train.

Drawing up between me and M. I
slow have life on ~~5~~ year old
child, with a childs ~~twenty~~
unconditions intensity. ~~Go ~~the~~
~~child appeared to~~ Between us
the years of unmix ~~rot~~ ROT
frustration and violence and
misery, I am 40 or younger and
~~you~~ scales by the blighting
of ~~unco~~ @ he has never known
~~be~~ Blighted x involves, serenity lost
forever. I don't take to myself
to freze D.P., corrupted and
brutalyzed by ~~the~~ years of
depression, ~~the~~ the years
in the Pens Colony, in D.P.
Camps, the brutalyzed ~~life~~
prison refs, violence, degradation,
hands torn from coldless
~~futile~~ ~~bodies~~ torn from
bordene wire, panting on

smiling like the
uncomplaining animal or
Christ, that has showed thy
sorrow. He knows all hardship
was in there from his birth
Nothing can frighten, quiet money —
but he will never change,
never matters, He can
learn translations, trembling,
how to circumvent, but
observations, acceptance,
mutuality he can never learn.
... bred with the years of
degradation and vice and
villainy, but the eyes still have
not things he loves, his eyes and
a ...
He soon learns as a ...
learns the customs of an
alien people. But he do not understand or
accept. He ...
He knows that Albertine does
not reciprocate, but he can not
withdraw or alter his

his own feelings. A young
a chap ~~[crossed out]~~ ~~[crossed out]~~
~~[crossed out]~~, his ~~[crossed out]~~
~~[crossed out]~~ hair; the ~~[crossed out]~~
~~[crossed out]~~ most masculine
~~[crossed out]~~ of allerton.

~~allerton does not want to
understand, because he cannot only
understand by living in the
R.P. [crossed out] himself.~~

the trip on the Evangeline train. You
~~[crossed out]~~ the ~~[crossed out]~~
~~[crossed out]~~
~~[crossed out]~~ him at his end the
half ~~[crossed out]~~ of a different arrival,
~~[crossed out]~~ Sunday and ~~[crossed out]~~ with
fear that he does not
understand or accept

56

Dream —   July 30

I arrived in San Jose. Red brick
suburbs. I said "This is nothing
but a picturesque fucking town."
Arrived at museum. I talked to
some one ~~who~~ there. Some sort
of expedition had been through
San Jose headed South. ~~He~~
~~described~~ "There were three" of them.
"One tall and thin." How old? I asked.
About 17? I described Allerton.
"Yes that's him." He asked about
their America." They flew down
to Ferrari - That's flooded out now,
No more planes can get in or out.
I felt good because Allerton
was trying to help me out with
information on Yage. Also explained
why he hadn't written. No mail
going out.

58

July 31,

A party. All there. He
seemed annoyed about something
Later I went back and the party
was over. I figured he had
gone to sleep in one of the rooms.
Waiting till 4 o'clock was no
because I was annoyed he had
said he gave M.S. of Malraux
to someone and had not done
so.

August 1

An address in Mexico for J.
A— Ito— Yo Mrs. Preston—
rent. Go to list. I was hurt
because he had not sent me
the address. Address was written on
a blue envelope in left hand
corner. [How now just how much it
would hurt if I got his
address from somebody else.. In a
way I would like to drop the
whole deal. Close the account.
But Friendly Finance never

In view of subsequent
discoveries in Peru, my ~~previous~~ earlier
conclusions ~~are~~ ~~subject of change,~~
~~are completely revised.~~ ~~are subject~~
Yoga subject to drastic alteration.

I made subsequent discoveries
~~about~~ about Yoga in Peru
in view of which ~~from~~ earlier
conclusions are completely revised.

certain goods, chattels, monies,
~~property~~ when in
charge or possession

The situation is getting worse.
Well this is what you ordered.
Isn't it? Some one not as ~~interchangeable~~,
interchangeable. Nothing was said in
the contract as to degree of reciprocity,
an affair being the only stipulation.
So like the Rosenberg's "What you have
sought have have obtained." Is this
the closest you can come to contact?
[Approach to complete interchangeability
is approach to no contact]. It can't.
No one can. It is precisely your own
hidden compromised ~~they~~ you want to
contact. It is in fact part of yourself.

August 3,
Ran into Phil Burton. Letter to Angela
all over S.A. the dream —. ~~Stopping~~
~~of putting~~ Did not show. I have a
feeling he is gone too. I'd like to
quit, close out A's account. But
Friendly Finance never turns love of
a client, or an agent.
Content.
The Party in the first part —

being of the human species, and ~~in condition~~ to this hereby does ~~agreement~~ agree to fullfill the terms of the contract as follows. clause 1 - [0 2 1 0 2 0 x] A - ~~the hereby agreed out for consideration after ... day P~~. Party in first Part - ~~receipt~~ for

August 4

No sign of Angelo. He's gone too. I hate Mexico, whole fuckin hemisphere. No wonder they took off from S. A. to the South Pacific. Ending up in the worst place of all. Easter Island and the fear of death. Fear of death is form of slow horror. The dead weight of time. An East is no slow horror because timeless.

Everything is delicious to me. Means to rain everything. Allerton. His darkness is a fraud, he is a squaw who

[All the foreigners out. Get out
expectiong suspicion, hostile cop.
a pale ghost of a courteous preserve
in the meaty room. Young indian
writes down the data. "Hey an
animal "
He ? face to face vicious meaty,
windy guy. What the matter with
that guy over there? I say, you
What do you want? I don't know.
What do you want. You no
Can't you make impossible? pointing
to misty canyon]
Swallowed the U.S.A. Customs
Con. whole. the a Representative
of this picturesque of culture
my hideous with pointless
conflict, stupid turmoil, a
sparks — adorable silence' couples
with the expansive respects of
a Nicks core. I ate the whole
fuckin hemisphere. How typical
american to go to bed with some
one ad resent it at the same time.

Everything has gone wrong here.
The question is why did they
ever leave in first place?
Something like the European
immigrant? Land of opportunity,
life — were all that shit?
Look at the emigrants who came
to American looking for a better
life. What they got now? If
they had the misfortune to
be successful one of the most
gruesome cultures ~~that~~ jackets
in history. ~~strange~~

Why the fear of the Foreigner? The
white Foreigner all S.A. can
pass without papers, but a
foreigner can not.

Last few days in Lima a nightmare.
The wind across the scabby huts.
~~a two days at the~~ I need
to get out of here.

[left margin, vertical text — illegible]

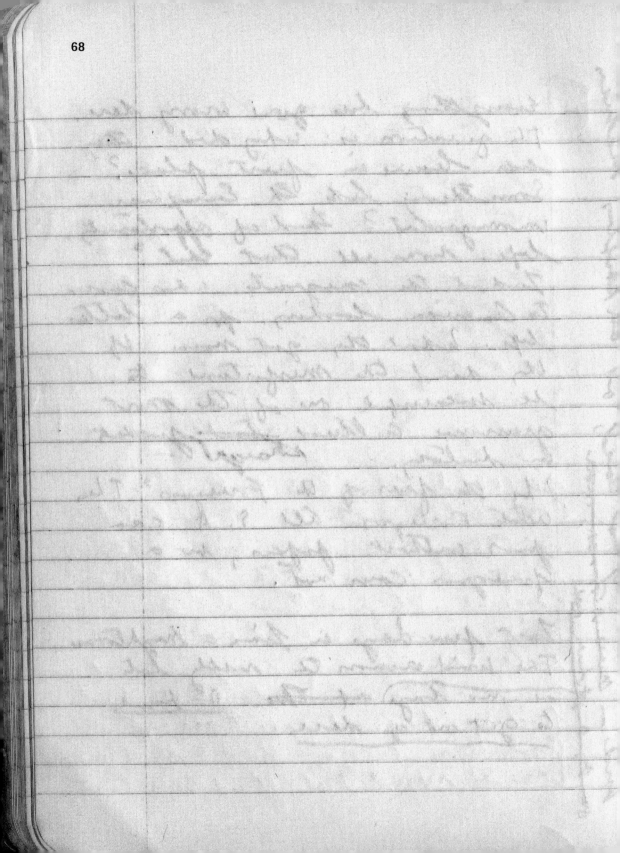

69

Last night dreamed of a
great ~~black~~ atomic Cloud
coming up from Chile spreading
a purple shadow over ~~Plaza~~
Zuñón, darker and darker. A
boy stands in the violet light,
and throws a jojo. He and
whistles an insolent little tune.
The ~~Chinamen~~ are shutting the doors
of their shops, pulling down
metal blinds.

A blind beggar plays a
sad high mountain tune on a
bamboo pipe, in the empty street.

The reformed drunk, the ~~grime~~
of portent crept the cook
complete, ~~Indian~~ reading a
detective story in an lumpy
arm chair, ~~on~~ ~~in a little~~
~~white~~ ~~an one were~~
~~in~~ ~~Polenapolas~~

A glass of ~~milk~~

The protest has failed. No place
to go, then. He pushed off as
worked out and slowed in a
circle and back. Here he is
finally as power where href
Indianapolis reading a detective
story in a lumpy arm
chair. Outside a November
rain and down the street the
neon lights of a Bar & Grill.
~~the end he saw that bonds~~
~~back to the arm chair.~~

It's like I came back to Mexico
City ~~years~~ after seeing
any 5 years absence of 5
Month. Everybody. Zong.

Can breaking Angela sharp and
Clear as overdue parties. Her
eyebrows. Her smile. The way
would stop when he saw me
with both hands in his
pocket his green sweater.

His ~~momentous~~ young male
gentleness, ~~one thanks to~~
~~fuckbox~~ ~~personal starting~~

Allerton Zone, Angelo gone.
Or where ~~has~~ I got? Not
even Yonge to Finlayson
a ~~reserve~~, a memory of
places DV² Anyhow it gave me
a ~~not certain~~ sensation ~~of~~ to
remember myself there.
"Angers had, All's spent"
It's almost two fat. Angelo
gone. He won the beer try &
July but, am I didn't know it.
I used to give him² $20.
now I would give him $100.
I want to help him.
No one else had of now
young male gentleness let an
affectionate aroused. ~~Total~~
~~turn of vacuousness~~ conflict
almost tauntly ~~in his~~ in his
freedom for vacuousness, hostility

Conflict.

"At Pearl. This is Yoga.
poetry. Just as there is word
music in painting in poetry.
I wonder if he has heard. I
wonder if it grows in South
Pacific.

Arthur has come home. His mother
~~you~~ ~~wife~~ has ~~gone~~ run off
with a traveling man. His
young wife ~~it~~ has gone
~~to~~ _____ with a ~~certain~~
~~m~~ _____. ~~he is~~ He is
~~regarded~~ devoting as to Pearl,
by Salem as the unequal
drunken, lunatic. ~~to get~~
"run, Jack, the white wale."
yeah." "Sure can I get had
an appointment."

Outside all pain. Meanwhile,
and like fog horns, as cars,
the city, and ~~team~~ no longer

home any place here.

What are they talking about.
Moslem and Christian? who
gives a fuck about religion.
I been to South America,
and S. out Pacific now
back here where we started from.
and this is the talk of children.
Moslem & Christian! God 3nd.
Do they believe all this
Well what about Allah?

Vera Cruz.
Hot and I feel a deep
discouragement. My mind goes
round and round ~~such times~~
repeating the same routines of
dull defensive clichés like a
nagging idiot. I see the S. A.
trip as a disaster that lost
me everything I had of value.
But if I keep floating back to me
like memories of a day time
nightmare. Slow traps. The

Mercado Margarita reveals full
grief and indifference by very
fact of tolerance. What is wrong
with S. A? ~~The~~ Disintegration into
component parts. The ~~neighboring~~
fear of death and age, you feel
dressing every day as something lost,
your flesh ages before your
eyes like a speed-up movie.
Control is growing like a cancer,
~~a~~ a ~~proliferating~~ proliferating ~~growth~~
Tumor of stupidity.
People just disappear. like in
the Margarita. You never see them
again. Angelo.
Here at night people swarm out and
walk round and round the
square.
The ideas are used and beaten
by the great meaningless ~~Connie~~.
The new world is a ~~great~~ lock
a yearning ache of despair. ~~a~~
deprivation and ~~crippling~~ shortage
the first conquest in the shrinking period

Dream — I was in Mexico City or ~~such~~ everywhere & looked such an ache of memories of Allerton and perhaps we have gone ~~away~~. I could not stay there. I must go now too. Angela went out sad, has ~~█████████~~ gone away somewhere. ~~I was~~ the way he used to help around this apt. out the hope I would help him, so now I want to and he is gone, ~~otherywhere~~ gone like Allerton, and Dave ~~anka~~ Jurado, and Juanac all the boys ~~they~~ ~~alive gay~~. ~~and~~ As if I had been away & gone. I am separated from them by a time gap. and especially from Marker.

Merida

~~Everybody here a most
pain in the ass they are
quickly~~ ...

as George it made things
any better to write about
them. Für sich das Ende
Dunkel ist dem Leben der? od
was. ... lyric only form
... meaning ...
... cry of pain. Meaning?
Simply

... R. Stein.
Why not just ... them? ...
... is this funny? ...
Clyde ... why is ...
... with ...
Why ... song then
... like ...
...

[illegible] appears – [illegible] – Spencer –
[illegible] come down – [illegible] –
[illegible] of Rome – [illegible] –
[illegible] – [illegible]
of [illegible] – [illegible] – [illegible] –
Dick – [illegible]

[illegible]

In your hide-out - Its much
way down yander in the gun
field - Missouri country - I'm from
Mo. - I gotta be shortly - oh
sorry when I AM
HERE IN this. PLaCE
Bill, I CAN NOT LeaF
PLEASE - Do not write
ME, BUT COME here
when you Receive this
- AS I need your
PROFESSIONAL
Atticatagnal
AddRess of Measure
For measure this
is A Real bad
Leaf, Bill, I AM
contin on your
Bonty mutiny on
the Bell string who
ever you are now
it is timely Aid
in, I must. have
light or ilse

96

After Sea giant junk — unappropriated
version — Fine trip to S.A. with
Allerton — Return to Mexico,
Left out — Allerton gives and
returns — Back to S.A. —
toward poor Allerton, S.A.
ships back to Mexico.
Everything lost —

Miami –
Panama –
Colombia –
The horrors

Bogota – new year
The Hill – the park –
beggars lined up – Snake
charmer – Spade lab
Back years later. there
is something –

F.O.B. Sea – Price no –
flights – I am not or
will not –

S. A. The giving up. the quitting.
the resignation,

He got on the plane ~~front~~,
his ~~duffle~~ ~~marked~~ ~~w~~

Panama and old Bill.

Ice

103

México, D. F.

Everybody gone. Old phe
disappeared, collection
gone, Angelo gone, my
banjos still on the Rim.
As if I had been away 5 years

fair copy

<u>Talara</u>   July 16.

A bus called <u>Proletario</u> just passed the bar where I am drinking my 5. P.M. rum. [Got to watch drinking I can black out on 4 drinks now.]

Trip up from Lima not too bad, as I shoved off with a tube of codeinetas and two nembies, and floated 12 hours. Rather a nice batch of Ecuadorians and Bolivians returning from Buenos Aires. Three times "all the foriegners" had to get out and register with the police. What do they do with these records. Use them as toilet paper I expect. Talara is in a desert that runs right down to the sea. Nothing grows here except a few watered palms around Company Houses. [This is a company town. Oil refinery.] Saw a terrible Spanish film. A woman representing death would appear now and then in a mist]. The audience laughed all through the film. Young kids mostly. Some incredible items on the hotel menu. "Lobsters cooked in whisky." "Scrambled children in piquant sauce." This is a misprint. I think they meant reñones not neños.

Last few days in Lima: Cold and damp. The Mercado Mayorista seems to have gone more or less sour. Saw a kid I propositioned. He looked <u>years</u> older. Last time I saw him he wasn't drinking. Now he drinks all the time. Knife scar under the left eye. Feel that everybody has gone <u>somewhere else</u>. The place isn't the same.

Tried to sell what I didn't want to take to the landlord. He gave me a low price on a few items, contracted to buy the rest the day I left at 9. A.M. By 3:30 he still hadn't showed. Figuring the gringo would leave that stuff for nothing. I gave most of it to an ice cream vendor.

Some to a gold toothed Chinese waiter, who was suspicious of the deal and did not thank me. Some people can't believe anyone is giving them anything.

July 17, Panama.

Ruins of 1910. Limed Trees – Wooden hospitals where people died in rows from yellow fever. Walked around with camera. People always know when you are taking their picture. Concept of soul loss. I was trying to get picture of young Indian on boat. Such languid animal inocence. He knew I was trying to take his picture and would always look up just as I was swinging camera into position. [Corrugated iron roofs, Wheeling albatrosses.

I got a batch of irradiation girls in from Hiroshima. "Just off the boat. Hot as a plutonium pile"]

Every cell vexes like junk sickness, what do I want from him? sitting leaning against the bow of the boat, idly scratching one shoulder — a long white scar on his right shoulder — looking up at me with a trace of sulkiness.

Walked around, started cooking. Need to see Angelo again.

Photography. There is something obscene here, a desire to capture, imprison incorporate.

What persistent pimps in Panama. One stopped me chewing my ear off about a 15 year old girl. I told him. "She's middle aged already. I want that 6 year old ass. Don't try palming your old 14 year old bats off on me."

Everyone here is telepathic on paranoid level. If you look at anyone he knows at once he is being observed and gives evidence of hostility and suspicion and restlessness.

[I represent the Friendly Finance Co. Haven't you forgotten something, Bill. Don't mind if I call you Bill do you? We like to keep on familiar terms with our clients. You've been a <u>bad</u> boy. <u>You know</u> you're supposed to come and see us every third Tuesday. We've been lonely for you in the office. <u>It hurts our feelings when a client skips out on us.</u> We're friendly folk, Louie, and we don't like to say pay up or else. Its not a friendly thing to say no matter how you slice it. I wonder if you ever read the contract, all of it. I have particular reference to clause 6 X which can only be deciphered with an electric microscope and a virus filter. I wonder if you know just what <u>or else</u> means, Louie? Ach I know how it is with you young kids. Careless, irresponsible, women, eh kid? They always give me the young ones because I know how to handle young kids: They all see the light and pay up, after a little heart to heart talk with old Uncle Willy.]

Aw I know how it is with you young. You get to chase after the floozies and forget about F. Friendly Finance don't you? But Friendly Finance doesn't forget you.

Like the song say No Hiding Place Down here. Not with skip tracer being on the job. They always give me the young ones, because I know how to handle young kids.

The inhabitants. A smog of bum kicks hangs over the town in the wet heat. The place has changed since I left, nothing but that awful hillbilly music on the juke boxes — Like the bellowings of a discontented cow, and the service men all look bovine and oddly blunted or brutalized as if they had received some special processing to fit them for peace time army life by a light concussion. You ask them a question and they answer it, and that is that. Conversation is impossible. They have nothing to say. They sit around buying drinks for the B girls like the stupid young jerks they are, and making mechanical passes without any real passion, just something to do, and playing that awful music. How could anyone be stupid enough to enjoy that bleating, whining crap. "It wasn't God made Honky Tonks," and "Youre driving Nails in My Coffin" and "Your Cheatin Heart."

[Last days in Lima. Nobody around the bars in the Mercado Mayorista. Nothing brings you down like you go in a place you used to like and there is nobody you know and everything is changed. The bar in a different place, the juke box moved, different waiters so you can't be sure you are in the same place. I suddenly decided to leave Lima at once, as if I had an urgent appointment somewhere else. This feeling of urgency has grown on me since I hit S. A. I have to be somewhere at a certain time. It seems vitally important to get the 1:30 PM plane and not wait over until 11 AM. The next day. In Guayquil I went to the house of the Peruvian Consul after his office hours so I could get a visa and leave one day early. Where am I going? Appointment in Talara, Tingo Maria, Pucallpa, Panama, Guatemala, Mexico? I don't know. Suddenly I have to leave right now.

[B girl in Chico's. Her shallow bird mind. Perfect English like a recording.

Mexico City.

Checked in Hotel and went straight to Tato's. No use asking Pepe for info. He wouldn't know where anybody was. I was looking only for one person. M. Like in a dream I had several times. I was back in Mexico talking to Eddie Wood or Louis Carpio. Then came the pause and we both drum on the table both knowing what I am going to say next. "Where is M?" Dream about M so many times. One dream takes me by arm and admitted I was a unique character." Usually we are on good terms but some times he is nasty and I keep asking why and never find out. Thursday going up to N. Y. to Enlist I in ambulance corps. Louie told me he is in Agua - Diente. South somewhere, and I ask when the bus leaves.] only one sex dream and I can't recall the details.] L. Carpio always there. First dream in back seat of car. Incredibly nasty. Later recognized rocks by road. Talk and I going north, I singing "Walking My Baby Back Home." Hotel Central and M. was in Peru? Question of

going back for more yage. Roads impassible. In restaurant. Beggar with withered hand —
Mitchell Tapachula.] Young U. S. offered him 10 c and would not take it. Another beggar
selling Colombian lottery tickets. . Young man with odd shirt — [Beads spangles] U.S. St.
Louis back yard. Saw him there in a bar. Reference to M. [He was in gangster hideout and
I went to find him.] Beggar info on M. Mitchell — Bone cancer. The H. Chase character. A
woman. Going back to Tapachula.

— Pucallpa.

Restaurant overrun with beggars and lots of foreigners back there now. When some
one said these are <u>Colombian</u> lottery tickets. No good here. He looked hurt and puzzled.
He never thought of that. Like M looks sometimes when I run on the point of American
friendship.

Sometimes I feel sorry for Allerton. He is such a child in a selfish, and callow sulky, and
sweet. But he doesn't realize what he is involved in. Like the pity I felt for my severed
finger, as if it was inocent victim of violent, unpredictable forces. Sometimes he looks
hurt and puzzled, by the warped intensity of my emotions. He wants my fucking, not a
relationship bordering on insanity.

A no more suited for this the part I anger him than I am suited to endure the fear or
pain and misery.

First in Tato's shook hands with Pepe- Talked the old retired regular army man. Asked
about M last. "By the way _ "

He didn't know M. Started walking around at random. Went into Sears and looked
at the magazines. Pictures of a lynching I see them Hang with bodies on A hand on my
shoulder. Gale. I ran through the list. All gone. M? I saw him about a month ago on the
other side of the street. It was like a main line shot of desolation, a cold spreading misery
that settles in the lungs and around the heart. I leaned against the magazine rack. "I'll see
you Gale." I walked out and leaned against a post. So he got all my letters. Why didn't he
answer Why? I walked down to 154. Looked in not a familiar face.

The pain inside sharp and definite as a physical wound. I walked back to Sears. Passed Gale and nodded. Back to Tato's. Talked to Mitchell. Eddie Wood, Crowley is all gone. Did you hear about M? No I said. He went down to S.A or some place with a colonel as a guide? "So" How long ago did he leave?" About six months ago. I could feel the pain ease a bit. "Must have been right after I left. "Yeah just about then." I got Carpio's address, and went over to see him. Met him as I was leaving the hotel. Yes M. left about 5 months ago and went along as guide to a Major and his wife. They were going to sell the car in Guatemala. A 47 buick. "I felt there was something a little wrong about the deal.

I could feel the pain switch off and on as I listened. What could he be doing and where? Guatemala is expensive. Just what was the deal. San Salvador etc expensive and jerk water. Costa Rica? Perhaps. I regretted not having visited San Jose on way up. "He said something about joining you down there." Evidently he had no beef against me. I felt better after talking to Louie.

Where is everybody? Eddie and Crowley and Johnny are in Calif. Russ and Johnny in Alaska. Like talking to Garver or some one like hitting the Times Square area. Where is everybody. So and So went wrong. So and so in jail. So and so dead from an overdose. J. oh he's still around. He's always around. Space - time travel across sands, the cold wind of change and death and the chance meeting. Mitchell with the missing fingers, Old Bill, the fresh winds of life and change, and a special significance. Nothing is happening completely by chance. There is the special significance to every meeting.

Looking for M.

I got out of the plane and waited for the tourist. "Lets take a cab into town. Split it. Cheaper that way". We walked through the airport like father and son. I took off my glasses and my hat was packed away in a suit case. I had my camera slung over my shoulder. Two tourists.

"Yes" I was saying "that old boy in Guatemala wanted to charge me $2.00 from the Palace Hotel out to the airport. I told him $1. "I held up a finger." No one looked at us. We got in a taxi. The driver said 12 for both.

"Wait a minute" the tourist said.

"No meter. Where is your meter. You got to have a meter."

The driver asked me to explain they were authorized to carry air line passengers without meter.

"No" he shouted. "Go on take me to the Regis. But I pay what is on the meter. Police. I call the Policía. Youre required to have a meter."

Oh God I thought. Thats all I need, this old Jerk should call the law. He was getting out of the car and taking down the number. "I call policia plenty quick" he said.

I said "Well I think I'll take this cab anyway, "vamonos" I said to the driver. We started on through the outskirts of Mexico, boys playing handball, trees and open lots I used to come this way every Monday to sign my bond. Back in Mexico City. The last chance acquaintance, picked up and dropped like a tool no longer useful I had left behind when he got out of the taxi. Back in Mexico City. From here on I would meet people who had the cryptic significance of a dream. Past orizaba Sears, "Here this will do". I checked into a 8 peso hotel. I walked out towards Tato's, my stomach cold with excitement like it was full of ice water. "Easy now. Cool. Cool. You have to be cool." The bar was in a different place. Redecorated. New furniture. But there was Pepe with his gold teeth and his moustache. 'Ah como esta?" he said. American". I looked at him speculating. Not much use asking him anything. I sat down with a delaware punch. The old Major walked in. Retired regular army. Grey haired vigorous, short. With him a young man I had seen before with another retired army man.

Dark, heavy beard, full red lips, handsome, I saw him walking around with Sarge carrying bundles. I figure the old Captain was picking up the check. A mooch, specializing in alcoholic army men with Pensions. Looking up from his beer with a silly grin, I ran through the list crisply with the Major. And last of all "What happened to M?" "I don't think I know him." Ah "well see you". I dropped 40 centavos on the table and walked out. Sears magazine counter. Sonny Goons — Gale. Retired army. All Gone. I never see those guys anyway. Never hang around in Tato's any more M? "Hes gone too" "How long ago? — No need to be casual he won't notice anything. "I saw him about a month ago on the other side of the street." A wave of misery and pain hit me like a main line shot, settling in the lungs and around the heart. Then I knew I was hung up on M. just the same as ever. I put the magazine away slowly, and walked outside and leaned against a post.

I was blocked from M by time gap. I missed the last train out of the Penal Colony, Everybody else gone. Chill of final desolation and despair: He must have got all the letters. Why didn't he answer why?

Stasis horrors. Not only I am never simple, but everyone else has gone

The winds of change and death dispersion and the seeing s††††,

A Cross roads of Space — Time travel the glory ††† ††††††.

winds of change and death, dispersion. A waiting room — where you grab a quick drink — before your train leaves. Cold fear of being left alone in the waiting room after all the trains had left.

Eddie Wood for Los Angeles —

? Russ and Johnny for Alaska via Houston. Betty and Jane for Tuscon. John for San Juan, Marker for - That's my train — where to? I can't hear you where to? His answer muffled by distance. I can't catch the name. Should I turn in my ticket? Dont be sure you'll never find him. You'll end up in a waiting room where the train don't stop anymore, the tracks grown over with weeds, playing checkers with the station masters with bottle tops playing bottle top checkers with the station master listening to the whistle of M's train fading in the distance, across the back yards, and red brick houses of St. Louis 1918. [The station master is setting up the bottle tops again].

"You're move." What is on my ticket I can't read it. Scrawled in red ink on yellow paper. Shall I turn it in? <u>wait for your own train.</u> [Lou Carpio and Pepe aren't waiting for him. They are in a joint] all the same people in room and in a for That is why you can stand to be in Mexico City or N.Y. because you are not stuck there. You are by the fact of being there, traveling. In Panama — cross road of the world — you are withering exactly

The citizens obviously stem from a line long line of pimps. M isn't the one Or ††††conscious or evil. They are just nowhere.

there, spirit innocence caught in aging cells and tissue. And you have to make the arrangements with P A N Am or the Dutch Line for removal of the body. Otherwise it would stay there and rot in the muggy heat under a galvanized iron roof and on a lime stone cliff over the stagnant bay where vultures eat fish entrails at low tide. Your train doesn't stop in Panama. In Lima only now and then and better not miss it. no schedule. You'd better be there when it leaves.

In Guatemala City maybe once in seven years. In Bogotá you can occasionally get a lift to your train in a Point 4 car. Ecuador has no service.

Note splits. Russ & Johnny. Betty and Jane. [Eddie to L.A. the last stop for U.S.D.P.S. Marker with the handsome con man and the youngish wife. Bill's waiting for the N. Y. train.

Time—Gap between me and M. I love him like a 4 year old child, with a childs unconditional intensity. Between us the years of inner rot frustration and violence and misery, I am year younger and older by the blighting of horrors he has never known. A Blighted inocense, serenity lost forever. I don't <u>believe</u> myself a psychic D. P., corrupted and brutilized by years of dispossession, the years in the Penal Colony, the D.P. Camp, the brutilized prison sex, vileness, degradation, hands torn from barbed wire, panting and snarling, the uncomprehending animal or child, that has learned the routine, he knows the barb wire is there from his torn hands — one finger joint missing — but he will never change never, <u>mature</u>. He can learn sometimes, thinking, how to circumvent, but resignation, acceptance, "maturity" he can never learn . Face is old with the years of degradation and vice and vileness, but the eyes slits look out through the wire; the eyes of a

He has learned as a tourist learns the customs of an alien people. But he did not understand or accept. He knows that Allerton does not reciprocate, but he can not withdraw or alter his own feeling. A yearning ache sullen — sweet muscular inocence of Allerton.

The lungs on the Pucallpa trail. Look at him with the half snarl of a baffled animal, snarling and whining with pain that he does not understand or accept.

Dream —   July 30

I arrived in San Jose. Red brick suburbs. I said, "This is nothing but a picturesque fucking town". Arrived at museum. I talked to some one there. Some sort of expedition had been through San Jose headed South. "There were three" of them. "One tall and thin." How old? I asked about 17? I described Allerton. "Yes that's him He asked about this Auaska.

They flew down to Ferrari — That's flooded out now.   No more planes can get in or out. I felt good because Allerton was trying to help me out with information on Yage. Also explained why he hadn't written. No mail going out.

[DRAWING]

July 31,

A party. All. there. He seemed annoyed about something. Later I went back and the party was over. I figured he had gone to sleep in one of the rooms. Waiting. till 6 o'clock or so because I was annoyed he had said he gave M.S. of malaria to some one and had not done so.

August 1

An address in Mexico for J. A.— Ihta — c/o Mr. Beaton — sent. to Art. I was hurt because he had not sent me the address. Address was written on a blue envelope in left hand corner. [know just how much it would hurt if I got his address from somebody else. In a way I would like to drop the whole deal. Close the account. But Friendly Finance never

In view of subsequent discoveries in Peru, my earlier conclusions Yage subject to drastic alteration.

I made subsequent discoveries about Yage in Peru in view of which earlier conclusions are completely invalid.

[EXCISED PAGE]

certain goods, chattels and services, including the charges and packing.

[4 LEAVES EXCISED, including facing page above]

The situation is getting worse. Well this is what you ordered. Isn't it? Some one not inter-changeable. Nothing was said on the contract as to degree of reciprocity: an affair being the only stipulation. So like the Rosenbergs'. "What you have sought has been obtained." Is this the closest you can come to contact? [Approach to complete <u>interchangeability</u> is approach to <u>no</u> contact]. if I can't. No one can. It is precisely <u>your own</u> hysteric confusion you want to contact. Is in fact part of <u>yourself.</u>

August 3,

Ran into Phil Benton. Letter to Angelo All over S. A. the dream _____. Did not show. I have a feeling he is gone too. I'd like to quit, close out A's account. But Friendly Finance never turns loose of a client, or an agent.

Contract.

   The Party in the first part ___ being of the human species, does hereby does agree to fulfill the terms of the contract as follows. Clause. 1 — [0 2 1 0 2 0 X] A. Party in first Part — for

August 4.

No sign of Angelo. He's gone too. I hate Mexico, whole fuckin hemisphere. No wonder they took off from S. A. to the South Pacific . Ending up in the worst place of all. Easter Island and the fear of death. Fear of death is form of stasis horrors. The dead weight of time. In East is no stasis horrors because timeless.

   Everything is detestable to me. Mexico the rain, everything. Allerton. His sweetness is a fraud, he is a square who

   [All the foriegnors out. Get out expecting suspicious, hostile cop. A pale ghost of a courteous presence in the misty room young Indian writes down the data. "Hay un animal."

H & H face to face across misty, windy gap. Whats the matter with that guy over there? I say you what do you want? I don't know. What do you want. You and Cant you see its impossible? pointing to misty canyon.]

Swallowed the U. S. A. culture con. whole. A representative of this miserable culture hideous with pointless conflict, stupid terrors, a spacho–somatic illness accepted with the cynical resignation of a sick cow. I hate the whole fuckin hemisphere. How typical American to go to bed with some one and resent it at the same time Everything has gone wrong here. The question is why did they ever leave in first place? Something like the European immigrant? Land of opportunity, life — room all that shit ? Look at the imigrants who come to America looking for a better life. What they got now. If they had the misfortune to be successful one of the most gruesome cultural straight jackets in history.

Why the fear of the Foriegnor? The white Foriegnor. All S. A. can pass without papers, but a foriegnor can not.

Last few days in Lima a nightmare The wind across the rubbly lots, and no boys inside — and damp and cold, and a shifting sickness. <u>I have to get out of here.</u>

Last night dreamed of a great atomic cloud coming up from Chile spreading a purple black shadow over Lima, darker and darker. A boy stands in the violet light, on a rising and throwing a jujo. and, whistles an insolent little tune. The Chinamen are shutting the doors of their shops, pulling down metal blinds.

A blind legless beggar plays a sad high mountain tune on a bamboo pipe in the empty street.

The reformed drunk, the years of protest over, the circle complete, back in Indiana reading a detective story in a lumpy arm chair.

The protest has failed. No place to go. He packed up and walked out and around in a circle and back. Here he is finally and forever soever here in Indianapolis reading a detective story in a lumpy arm chair. Outside a November rain and down the street the neon lights of a Bar & Grill.

It's like I came back to Mexico City after being away 5 years instead of 5 months. Everybody. Gone.

Can visualize Angelo sharp and clear as overdue pusher. His eye brows. His smile. The way would stop when he saw me with both hands in his pocket his green sweater. His young male gentleness,

Allerton Gone, Angelo gone. And what have I got? Not even yage. visualize a sickness. The memory of places so awful it gives me a sinking sensation to remember myself there. "Naughts had, all's spent." M is almost too pat. Angelo gone. He was the best boy I ever had, and I didn't know it. I used to give him $20. Now I would give him $100. I want to help him. No one else had the same young male gentelness like an affectionate animal. Almost saintly in his freedom from viciousness, hostility, conflict.

St-Perse. This is Yage. poetry. Just as there is weed music and painting and poetry. I wonder if he ever used it. I wonder if it grows in South Pacific.

Ahab has come home. His mistress has run off with a traveling man. His young wife has gone to _____ with a certain Mr. _____. He is avoided on the Bounty by Sailors as an incompetent drunken, lunatic. Sure, Jack., the white wale .. yeah .. Scuse me I got like an appointment"

Outside in the rain. Trainwhistle, and like fog horns, and cars, The City, and no longer have any place here.

What are they talking about Moslem and Christian? Who gives a fuck about religion. I been to South America. and South Pacific now back here where we started from. all this is the talk of children. Moslem & Christian! God said. Do they believe all this bull shit about Allah?

Vera Cruz.

Hot and I feel a deep discouragement. My mind goes round and round repeting the same routine of dull defensive cliches like a nagging idiot. I see the S. A. trip as a disaster that lost me everything I had of value. Bits of it keep floating back to me like memories of a day time nightmare. Slow traps. The Mercado Mayorista reveals full gap and indifference by very fact of tolerance. What is wrong with S.A? Disintegration into component parts. The nightmare fear of death and age, you feel every day as something lost, your flesh ages before your eyes like a speed up movie, Control is growing like a cancer, a proliferating Tumor of stupidity.

People just disappear. Like in the Mayorista. You never see them again. Angelo.

Here at night people swarm out and walk round and round the square. The Indians are sad and beaten by the great meaningless country. The New World is a lack a yearning ache of despair. deprivation and shrinkage. The fish caught in the shrinking pond

Dream. I was in Mexico City and everywhere I looked such an ache of memories of Allerton and people who have gone away. I could not stay there. I must go now too. Angelo sweet and sad, has gone away somewhere. The way he used to help around the apt. and he hoped I would help him, and now I want to and he is gone, inexplicably gone like

Allerton, and Dave and Jurado, and Juan and all the boys . As if I had been away 5 years. I am separated from them by a time gap. and especially from Marker.

Merida.

The — Iam as he — R. Stern. Why not just hang them? Like in Oran — Is this for my sake? Clyde Gardinier — What is word for Con in Spanish? Gale likes aspirin with codiene. Why. I was sorry then. I don't like abstraction. The reward — homicide squad, by hemp. like Ahab. John Brown. The white whale — I have lost ___. St. Louis tragic affairs. Joan. Mrs. Spencer Let it come down — I wunderbar The Last Annals of Rome — Vidal — Damaged to the soul — the news of Marker — Harry — Tom — Dick —

[NEXT FOUR LEAVES CONTAIN
ASEMIC WRITING AND DRAWINGS]

G's hide-out — Not much way down yonder in the green field — Missouri cruelty — I'm from Mo, — I gotta be showdby Oh Lord. When I AM HeRE IN this . PLACe Bill, I CAN NOT LeaF PleASe — Do not write Me, BUT COMe Here when yoo Receive this T — AS I Need your professionalAL AttentionAL Kindees of Measure FOR Measure this is A Real bad deal, Bill, I AM CONTIN ON YOUR BONTY MUTINY ON The Bell string Who ever you are now it is timely Aid IN I MUSt HAVe light oR eLSe ?

When Lee quit junk — unexpurgated version — First trip to S. A with Allerton. Return to Mexico, Left out — Allerton goes and returns — Back to S. A. No word from Allerton, S. A trip and back to Mexico.

Everything lost —

<u>Miami</u>–
Panama —
Colombia —
The horror

[DRAWING]

Bogota — Green grass
The Hill — the park —
beggars lined up — Snake Charmer. Spider lal
Back <u>years</u> latter. There is some thing —

L. B. Lee — In or ✝✝ — blighted — I can not or will not ——

[TWO DRAWINGS]

S. A. The giving up. The quiting. The resignation,

He got on the plane a little drunk his clothes soaked with [DRAWING]

Panama and old Bill —

Lee

Mexico, D. F.

Everybody gone. Old Ike disappeared, Allerton gone, Angelo gone, my lawyer still on the lam. as if I had been away 5 years.

(with notes and variant readings)

Page 3

<u>Talara</u>   July 16 .

A bus called <u>Proletario</u> just passed the bar where I am drinking my 5. P.M. rum. [Got to watch drinking I can black out on 4 drinks now.]

Trip up from Lima not too bad, as I shoved off with a tube of codeinetas[1] and two nembies, and floated 12 hours. Rather a nice batch of Ecuadorians and Bolivians returning from Buenos Aires. Three times "all the foriegners"[2] had to get out and register with the police. What do they do with these records. Use them as toilet paper I expect. Talara is in a desert that runs right down to the sea. Nothing grows here except a few watered palms around Company Houses. [This is a company town. Oil refinery.[3]] Saw a terrible Spanish film. A woman representing death would appear now and then in a

Pages 4–5

mist]. The audience laughed all through the film. Young kids mostly. Some incredible items on the hotel menu. "Lobsters cooked in whisky." "Scrambled children in piquant sauce." This is a misprint. I think they meant reñones not neños.[4]

Last few days in Lima: Cold and damp. The Mercado Mayorista seems to have gone more or less sour. Saw a kid I propositioned. He looked <u>years</u> older. Last time I saw him he wasn't drinking. Now he drinks all the time. Knife scar under the left eye. Feel that everybody has gone <u>somewhere else</u>. The place isn't the same.

Tried to sell what I didn't want to take to the landlord. He gave me a low price on a few items, contracted to buy the rest the day I left at 9. A. M. By 3:30 he still hadn't showed. Figuring the gringo would leave that stuff for nothing. I gave most of it to an ice cream vendor.

---

1. "codeinetas" appears as "codeineetas" in *Yage Letters Redux,* edited by Oliver Harris (San Francisco: City Lights, 2006, p. 59); *Naked Lunch: The Restored Text,* edited by James Grauerholz and Barry Miles (New York: Grove, 2003, p. 41).
2. **foriegners** [*sic*], i.e., foreigners
3. Oil **refining**
4. **reñones** [*sic*], i.e., riñones; **neños** [*sic*], i.e., niños. *Riñones* and *niños* mean kidneys and children, respectively.

Pages 6–7

Some to a gold toothed Chinese waiter, who was suspicious of the deal and did not thank me. Some people can't believe anyone is giving them anything.

July 17, Panama.

‡ Ruins of 1910. Limed Trees – Wooden hospitals where people died in rows from yellow fever.[5] Walked around with camera. People always know when you are taking their picture. Concept of soul loss. ~~Through pict~~. I was trying to get picture of young Indian on boat. Such languid animal inocence.[6] He knew I was trying to take his picture and would always look up just as I was swinging camera into position. [Corrugated iron roofs, ~~people living in~~. Wheeling albatrosses. Every cell vexes[7] like junk sickness, what do I want from him? sitting leaning against the

---

Pages 8–9

I got a batch of irradiation girls in from Hiroshima. "Just off the boat.[8] Hot as a plutonium pile"]

bow of the boat, idly scratching one shoulder — a long white scar on his right shoulder — looking up at me with a trace of ~~sulleness~~ sulkiness. Walked around, started cooking. Need to see Angelo again.

Photography. There is something obscene here, a desire to capture, imprison ~~the~~ incorporate.

What persistent pimps in Panama[9] One stopped me chewing my ear off about a 15 year old girl. I told him. "She's middle aged already. I want that 6 year old ass. Don't try palming your old 14 year old bats off on me."

Everyone here is telepathic on paranoid level. If you look at anyone he knows at once he is being observed and gives evidence of hostility and suspicion and restlessness.

---

5. **Yellow fever** had effectively been controlled in Panama by 1910.
6. **inocence** [*sic*], i.e., innocence
7. Every **one** vexes
8. off **a** boat
9. **Panama** [*sic*], i.e., **Panama.**; see fair copy, page 107.

Pages 10–11

^Its not a friendly thing to say ^no matter how you slice it.

[I represent the Friendly Finance Co. Haven't you forgotten something, Bill. Don't mind if I call you Bill do you? We like to keep on familiar terms with our clients. You've been a <u>bad</u> boy. <u>You know</u> you're supposed to come and see us every third Tuesday. We've been lonely for you in the office. <u>It hurts our feelings when a client skips out on us.</u>[10] We're friendly folk, Louie, and we don't like to say pay up or else. ^[11] I wonder if you ever read the contract, all of it. I have particular reference to clause 6 X which can only be deciphered with an electric microscope and a virus filter. I wonder if you know just what <u>or else</u> means, Louie?

Ach I know how it is with you young kids. Careless, irresponsible, ^*women, eh kid?* They always give me the young ones because I know how to handle young kids: They all see the light and pay

Pages 12–13

up, after a little heart to heart talk with ~~Bill~~ old Uncle Willy.] ~~Yes sir I never had to have to~~

Aw I know[12] how it is with you young. ~~kids~~[13] You get to chase after the floozies a[14] forget about ~~us the~~ F. Friendly Finance ~~eh kid,~~ don't you? But Friendly Finance ~~doesn~~ doesn't forget you. ~~Like the song say "Learning to love from now on"~~

Like the song say No Hiding Place Down here. Not with skip tracer being on the job. They always give me the young ones, because I know how to ~~talk~~ handle young kids.

---

10. **It hurts . . . out on us.** Editors cannot determine if this passage is underlined or excised.

11. (from margin): **Its** [*sic*], i.e., It's

12. **Ah** I know . . .

13. ~~kids~~ is an erasure.

14. **a** [*sic*], i.e., **and**; see fair copy, page 107.

Pages 14–15

The inhabitants. A smog of bum kicks hangs over the town in the wet heat. ~~Saw a picket demanding jobs for Panamanian sea men.~~

~~In~~ The place ~~had~~ has changed since I left, ~~a time~~ nothing ~~everything~~ but that awful hillbilly music on the juke boxes — Like the bellowings of a discontented cow, and th[15] service men all look bovine and oddly blunted or brutalized as if they had received some special processing to fit them for peace time army life ^by a light concussion.[16] You ask them a question and they answer it, and that is that. Conversation is impossible. They have nothing to say. They sit around buying drinks for the B girls like the stupid young jerks they are, and making mechanical passes without any real passion, just something to

Pages 16–17

do, and playing that awful music. How could anyone be stupid enough to enjoy that bleating, whining crap. "It wasn't God made Honky Tonks," and "Youre[17] driving Nails in My Coffin" and "Your Cheatin Heart."

[Last days in Lima. Nobody around the bars in the Mercado Mayorista. Nothing brings you down like you go in a place you used to like and ~~nobody~~ there is nobody you know and everything is changed. The bar in[18] a different place, the juke box moved, different waiters so you can't be sure you are in the same place. I suddenly decided to leave Lima <u>at once</u>, as if I ~~was hot with the law or~~ had an <u>urgent appointment somewhere else.</u> This feeling of urgency has grown on me since I hit S. A. I <u>have</u> to be somewhere

---

15. **th** [*sic*], i.e., **the**; see fair copy, page 107.
16. life **in** a light
17. **"Youre** [*sic*] . . .", i.e., "You're . . ."
18. bar **is** a different

Pages 18–19

at a certain time. It seems vitally important to get the 1:30 P M plane and not wait over until 11 A M. The next day. In Guayquil[19] I went to the house of the Peruvian Consul after his office hours so I could get a visa and leave one day early. Where am I going? Appointment in Talara, Tingo Maria, Pucallpa, Panama, Guatemala, Mexico? I don't know. Suddenly I <u>have</u> to leave <u>right now</u>.

[B girl in Chico's. Her shallow bird mind. Perfect English like a recording.

<u>Mexico City</u>.

~~Wen~~ Checked in Hotel and went straight to Tato's. No use asking Pepe for info. He wouldn't know where anybody was. I was looking only for one person. M. Like in a dream I had several times.

Pages 20–21

one[20] dream
takes me by arm
and admitted
I was a unique
character"[21, 22]

I was back in Mexico talking to Eddie Wood or Louis Carpio. Then came the pause and we both drum on the table both knowing what I am going to say ^next. "Where is M?" Dream about M so many times. Usually we are on good terms but some times he is nasty and I keep asking why and never find out. Thursday going up to N. Y. to Enlist I in ambulance corps. Louie told me he is in Agua - Diente. South somewhere, and I ask when the bus leaves.]   only one sex dream and I can't recall the details.] L. Carpio always there. First dream in back seat of car. Incredibly nasty. Later recognized rocks by road. Talk and I going north, I singing "Walking My Baby Back Home." Hotel Central and M.

---

19. **Guayquil** [*sic*], i.e., Guayaquil

20. **one** [*sic*], i.e., **One**; see fair copy, page 108.

21. **character"** [*sic*], i.e., **character.";** see fair copy, page 108.

22. Editorial decision to insert **One dream . . . character"** from facing page into main text. The passage is judged integral to the narrative; see fair copy, page 108.

Pages 22–23

Mitchell

was in Peru? Question of going back for more yage. Roads impassible. In restaurant. Beggar with withered hand — ∧ Tapachula.] Young U. S. offered him 10 c and would not take it. Another beggar selling Colombian lottery tickets. . Young man with odd shirt — [Beads spangles] U.S. St. Louis back yard. Saw him there in a bar. Reference to M. [He was in gangster hideout and I went to find him.] Beggar info on M. Mitchell — Bone cancer. The H. Chase character. A woman. Going back to Tapachula. —Pucallpa.

Restaurant overun[23] with beggars and lots of forigners[24] back there now. When ~~it u~~ some one said these are <u>Colombian</u> lottery tickets. No good here. He looked ~~a~~ hurt and puzzled. He never thought of that. Like M looks sometimes when I run on the point of American friendship.[25]

Page 24

Sometimes I feel sorry for Allerton[26] He is such a child in a ~~way, and he~~ selfish, and callow ~~ad~~ sulky, and sweet. But he doesn't ~~want~~ realize what he is involved in. Like the pity I felt for my severed finger, as if it was inocent[27] victim of violent, unpredictable forces. Sometimes he looks hurt and puzzled, by the ~~inten~~ warped intensity of my emotions. He wants my fucking, not a relationship bordering on insanity.

A[28] no more suited for this the part I anger[29] him than I am suited[30] to endure the fear or pain and misery.

---

23. **overun** [*sic*], i.e., overrun
24. **forigners** [*sic*], i.e., foreigners
25. **American friendship** is a best guess by Editors.
26. **Allerton** [*sic*], i.e., **Allerton.**; see fair copy, page 109.
27. **inocent** [*sic*], i.e., innocent
28. **A** [*sic*], i.e., Allerton
29. I **imagine** him
30. **sentenced** to endure

Page 25

First in Tato's shook hands with Pepe- Talked the old retired regular army man. Asked about M last. "By the way _   "

He didn't know M. Started walking around at random. Went into Sears and looked at the magazines. Pictures of a lynching I see them Hang with bodies on A hand on my shoulder. Gale. I ran through the list. All gone. M? I saw him about a month ago on the other side of the street. ~~I felt a~~ It was like a main line shot of desolation, a cold spreading misery that settles in the lungs and around the heart. I leaned against the magazine rack. "I'll see you Gale." I walked out and leane[31] against a post. So he got all my letters. Why didn't he answer Why? I walked down to 154. Looked in not a familiar face.

Pages 26–27

The pain inside sharp and definite as a physical wound. I walked back to Sears. Passed Gale and nodded. Back to Tato's. Talked to Mitchell. Eddie Wood, Crowley is all gone. Did you hear about M? No I said. He went down to S.A or some place with a colonel as a guide? "So" How long ago did he leave?" About six months ago. I could feel the pain ease ~~up~~ a bit. "Must have been right after I left. "Yeah just about then." I got Carpio's address, and went over to see him. Met him as I was leaving the hotel. Yes M. left about 5 months ago and went along as guide to a Major and his wife. They were going to sell the car in Guatemala. A 47 buick. "I felt there was something a little wrong about the deal.

---

31. **leane** [*sic*], i.e., **leaned**; see fair copy, page 109.

Pages 28–29

I could feel the pain switch off and on as I listened. ~~to~~ What could he be doing and where? Guatemala is expensive. Just what was the deal. San Salvador etc expensive and jerk water. Costa Rica? Perhaps. I regretted not having visited San Jose[32] on way up. "He said something about joining you down there." Evidently he had no ~~comp~~ beef against me. I felt better after talking to Louie.

Where is everybody? Eddie and Crowley and Johnny are in Calif.? Russ and Johnny in Alaska. Like talking to Garver or some one like hitting the Times Square area. Where is everybody. So and So went wrong. So and so in jail. So and so dead from an overdose. J. oh he's still around. He's always around. ~~The yage feel of~~ Space - time travel across sands,[33] the cold wind of

Pages 30–31

change and death and the chance meeting. Mitchell with the missing fingers, Old Bill, the fresh winds of ~~damage and death~~ life and change, and ~~the~~ a special significance. ~~of chance meetings.~~ Nothing is happening completely by chance. There is the special significance to every meeting.

---

32. **Jose** [*sic*], i.e., José
33. across **winds,** the cold

Pages 32–33

Looking for M.

I got out of the plane and waited for the tourist. ~~to collect his hat and wide straw hat — bought in Guatemala — and his hand bag and his camera~~, "Lets[34] take a cab into town. Split it. Cheaper that way". We walked through the airport like father and son. I took off my glasses and my hat was packed away in a suit case. I had my camera slung over my shoulder. Two tourists.

"Yes" I was saying "that old boy in Guatemala wanted to charge ~~us~~ $2.00 ~~to~~ ^{me} from the Palace Hotel out to the airport. I told him $1. "I held up a finger." ~~But he say no. This~~ No one looked at us. ~~except cab drivers~~ We got in a taxi. The driver said 12 for both.

"Wait a minute" the tourist said.

Pages 34–35

"No meter. Where is your meter. You got to have a meter." The driver asked me to explain they were authorized to carry air line passengers without meter.

"No" he shouted. "Go on take me to the Regis. But I pay what is on the meter. Police. I call the Policía. Youre[35] required to have a meter."

Oh God I thought. Thats[36] all I need, ~~is the~~ this old Jerk should call the law. He was getting out of the car and taking down the number. "I call policia[37] plenty quick" he said.

I said "Well I think I'll take this cab anyway, "vamonos"[38] I said to the driver. We started on through the outskirts of Mexico, boys playing handball,[39] trees and open lots ~~and Mo~~ I used to come this way every Monday to

---

34. **"Lets** [*sic*], i.e., "Let's
35. **Youre** [*sic*], i.e., You're
36. **Thats** [*sic*], i.e., That's
37. **policia** [*sic*], i.e., policía
38. **vamonos** [*sic*], i.e., vámonos
39. playing **baseball**, trees

Pages 36–37

sign my bond. Back[40] in Mexico City. The last chance acquaintance, picked up and dropped like a tool no longer useful I had[41] left behind when he got out of the taxi. Back in Mexico City. ~~Here~~ From here on ~~people~~ I would meet people who had the cryptic significance of a dream. Past orizaba[42] ~~back~~ Sears, "Here this will do". I checked into a 8 peso hotel. I walked out towards Tato's, my stomach cold with excitement like it was full of ice water. "Easy now. Cool. Cool. You have to be cool." The bar was in a different place. Redecorated. New furniture. But there was Pepe with his gold teeth and his moustache. ~~Oh~~ 'Ah como esta?"[43] ~~h?~~ he said. American". I looked at him speculating.[44] Not much use asking him

Pages 38–39

anything. I sat down with a delaware punch.[45] ~~He's~~ The old Major walked in. Retired regular army. Grey haired vigorous, short. With him a young man I had seen before with another retired army man. ~~Heavy beard, full lips, and handsome in a 1920, lowlife way.~~[46]

Dark, heavy beard, full red lips, handsome, ~~traveling with some one trailing after the man's pension.~~ I saw him walking around with Sarge carrying bundles. I figure the old Captain was picking up the check. A ~~specialized~~ mooch, specializing in alcoholic army men with Pensions. Looking up from his beer with a silly grin, I ran through the list crisply with the Major. And last of all "What happened to M?" "I don't think I know him."

---

40. bond. **Bonds** in Mexico
41. I **have** left
42. **orizaba** [*sic*], i.e., Orizaba. Burroughs had lived in Apartment 5 at 210 Orizaba, in the Colonia Roma, from June 1951 until he left Mexico City in December 1952.
43. **'Ah como esta?"** [*sic*], i.e., "Ah cómo está?"
44. him **speaking**. Not
45. **delaware punch** [*sic*], i.e., Delaware Punch, a fruit flavored soft drink from the early twentieth century and still sold in Texas.
46. ~~lowlife way~~ is a best guess by Editors.

Pages 40–41

Ah "well see you". I dropped 40 centavos on the table and walked out. Sears magazine counter. Sonny Goons – Gale. Retired army. All Gone. I never see those guys anyway. Never hang around in Tato's any more " M? "Hes[47] gone too?" "How long ago? – No need to be casual he won't notice anything. "I saw him about a month ago on the other side of the street." ~~It I felt like a main line shot of a cold spreading~~ A ~~cold~~ wave of misery and pain ~~settled~~ hit me like a main line shot, ~~and~~ settling in the lungs and around the heart. Then I knew I was hung up on M. just the same as ever. I put the magazine away slowly, and walked outside and leaned against a post. ~~It was like missing the train, everybody had gone away and left me~~

Pages 42–43

Stasis horrors. Not only I am never simple,[48] but everyone else has gone

~~Like I~~ I was blocked ~~separate~~ ~~separated~~ from M by ~~a~~ time gap. ~~Left completely alone in a time and place where I felt like I had~~ I missed the last train out of the Penal Colony, Everybody else ~~was on the train~~ gone. ~~A~~ Chill of final desolation and despair: He must have all got[49] the letters[50] Why didn't he answer why? ~~Something else was more important~~

¥ The winds of change and death dispersion and the seeing s++++,

A Cross roads of Space –Time travel ^ ~~the him th~~ winds of change and death, dispersion. A waiting room – where you grab a quick drink[51] – before ~~the~~ your train leaves. Cold fear of being left alone in the waiting room after all the trains had left.

^ the glory +++ ++++++.

---

47. **Hes** [*sic*], i.e., He's
48. **simple** is a best guess by the Editors.
49. Transcription **must have all got** emended to **must have got all** in fair copy, page 112.
50. **letters** [*sic*], i.e., **letters.**; see fair copy, page 112.
51. quick **dinner**

Eddie Wood for Los Angeles —

? Russ and Johnny[52] for Alaska via Houston. Betty and Jane for Tuscon.[53] John for San Juan,

---

Pages 44–45

playing bottle top checkers with the station master <

Marker for -   That's my train — where to? I can't hear you where to? ~~He is always on the train and I cant hear the r~~ His answer muffled by distance. I can't catch the name. Should I turn in my ticket? Dont[54] be sure[55] you'll never find him. ~~If you keep looking   Because he isn't where you~~ You'll end up in a waiting room ~~somewhere with no tr~~ ~~like Mexico~~ where the train don't stop anymore, the tracks grown over with weeds, ~~and the insane station master calls out~~ playing ~~eternal~~ checkers with the station masters with bottle tops[56] ᴧ listening to the whistle of M's train fading in the distance, across the back yards, and red brick houses, ~~of St. Louis 1918.~~ of St. Louis 1918. [The station master is setting up the bottle top again].

Pages 46–47

~~with the~~ all the same people ~~++++ for the~~ in room and in a for,[57]

red

"You're move."   What is on my ticket I can't read it. Scrawled in ~~yellow~~ ink Shall I turn it in? ~~Better~~ wait for your own train. on yellow paper.[58] ~~Lou Carpio and Pepe, are still Lou Carpio bought~~ [Lou Carpio and Pepe aren't waiting for him. They are in a joint] That is why you can stand to be in Mexico City or N.Y. because you are not stuck there. You are by the fact of being there, ~~— you being somewhere else~~ traveling.

---

52. **Ron** and **Jim** for Alaska
53. **Tuscon** [*sic*], i.e., Tucson.
54. **Dont** [*sic*], i.e., Don't
55. **silly** you'll never
56. **top** [*sic*], i.e., **tops**; see fair copy, page 112.
57. **all the same people . . . for** inserted into fair copy, page 112; see also facsimile. The reading is unclear, but **people** is our best guess.
58. **on yellow paper** inserted into fair copy, page 112; see also facsimile.

In Panama — ~~The so called~~ cross road of the world — ~~There is no feel of travel—~~
you are ~~jus~~ withering[59] exactly[60] there, ~~like a~~ spirit ~~caught,~~ in ~~dying~~ aging ~~++~~ - ^{innocence caught} ^{sign}
~~tissue tissue~~ cells and tissue.. And you have to make ^{the} arrangements with P A N Am or
the Dutch Line for removal of the body.

Pages 48–49

~~the people~~

p ++++++ ++++
The citizens ~~of this~~
~~town/~~ obviously ~~come~~
~~from~~ stem from a line
~~long~~ long line of pimps.
~~They~~   M isn't the one
Or ++++ conscious or evil.
They are just nowhere.

Otherwise it would stay there and rot~~s~~ in the muggy heat
under a galvanized iron roof and on ~~on~~ a ~~dry, cliff~~ lime
stone cliff over the stagnant bay where vultures eat fish
entrails at low ~~tides.~~ tide. ~~You can't wait for your train.~~
~~Get any train~~ out ~~of there.~~   Your train doesn't stop in
Panama. ~~Any ++~~ In Lima only now and then and better not
miss it. ˄[61] In Guatemala City maybe once in seven years.
In Bogotá you can occasionally[62] get a lift to your train in a
Point 4[63] car. Ecuador has no service.

   Note splits. Russ & Johnny. Betty and Jane. [Eddie to
L..A.. the ~~final nightmare of +++++ of~~ last stop for U.S.D.P.S.[64]
Marker with the handsome con man and the youngish wife. Bill's
~~watery blue eyes turning towards N. Y. like a sea side~~

< no schedule. You'd better be there when it leaves

---

59. are **unknown** exactly
60. withering **back** there; withering **wreck** there
61. **no schedule . . . leaves**: inserted from margin into fair copy, page 112.
62. can **usually** get
63. **Point 4**, i.e., Point Four Program of Technical Assistance to Developing Nations, which was a U.S. governmental program proposed by President Truman in his 1949 Inaugural Address and later enacted by Congress.
64. **U.S.D.P.S.** is an apparent acronym for a displaced persons program, but an exact program matching the acronym has not been identified.

Pages 50–51

unconditional

~~bird blown~~

waiting for the N. Y. train.

Time—Gap between me and M. I love him like a 4 year old child, with a childs[65] ~~intensity~~ ∧ uncondition[66] intensity. ~~Only like death experience is~~ Between us the years of inner ~~rot,~~ rot frustration and violence and misery, I am year younger ~~and~~ and ~~year~~ older by the blighting of horrors he has never known. A[67] Blighted, inocense,[68] serenity lost forever. I don't <u>believe</u>[69] myself a psychic D. P., corrupted and brutilized[70] by ~~the~~ years of dispossession, ~~and~~ the years in the Penal Colony, the D.P. Camp, the brutilized~~sex~~ prison sex, vileness, degradation, ~~hands torn from countless futile~~ hands torn from barbed wire, panting and

Pages 52–53

snarling, ~~like~~ the uncomprehending animal or child, that has learned the routine, he knows the barb wire is there from his torn hands — one finger joint missing — but he will never change never, <u>mature</u>. He can learn sometimes, thinking, how to circumvent, but resignation, acceptance,[71] "maturity" he can never learn . Face is old with the years of degradation and vice and vileness, but the eyes slits look out through the wire; the eyes of a

---

65. **childs** [*sic*], i.e., child's
66. **unconditional** from the top margin has replaced **uncondition** in the fair copy, page 113; see also facsimile.
67. **A**, from margin, seemingly added later.
68. **inocense** [*sic*], i.e., innocence
69. don't <u>liken</u> myself
70. **brutilized** [*sic*], i.e., brutalized
71. resignation, **accepting**

He ~~can~~ ^{has} learned[72] as a ~~stranger~~ ^{tourist} learns the customs of an alien people. But he did not understand or accept. ~~He is patient, and~~ He knows that Allerton does not reciprocate, but he can not withdraw ~~the~~ or alter his[73]

Pages 54–55

~~to bed~~

his own feeling. A yearning ache ~~++++ Allerton's ribs and hands and stomach, his eyebrows and brown hair, the whole sweet~~ sullen - sweet muscular inocence[74] of Allerton. ~~Allerton does not~~ <u>want</u> ~~to understand, because he could only understand by living in the camp D.P. camp himself.~~

The lungs on the Pucallpa trail. ~~My breath short, the ache in the lungs I caught my hands shaking though my tulla.~~[75] Look at him with the half snarl of a baffled animal, ~~snarl~~ snarling and whining with pain that he does not understand or accept.

Pages 56–57

Dream –   July 30

I arrived in San Jose.[76] Red brick suburbs. I said, "This is nothing but a picturesque fucking town". Arrived at museum. I talked to some one ~~who~~ there. Some sort of expedition had been through San Jose[77] headed South. ~~He described~~ "There were three" of them. "One tall and thin." How old? I asked about 17? I described Allerton.

---

72. **had** learned
73. Apparent repetition of **his**; second "his" deleted from fair copy, see page 113.
74. inocence [*sic*], i.e., innocence
75. **tulla**: Volume editor Oliver Harris notes that the word *tulla* is defined in "In Search of Yage," as a "rubber bag."
76. **Jose** [*sic*], i.e., José
77. **Jose** [*sic*], i.e., José

"Yes that's him *" He asked about this Auaska.[78] *" They flew down to Ferrari — That's flooded out now.   No more planes can get in or out. I felt good because Allerton was trying to help me out with information on Yage. Also explained why he hadn't written. No mail going out.

[DRAWING]

Pages 58–59

July 31,

A party. All.[79] there. He seemed annoyed about something. Later I went back and the party was over. I figured he had gone to sleep in one of the rooms. Waiting. till 6 o'clock or so because I was annoyed he had said he gave M.S. of malaria to some one and had not done so.

August 1

An address in Mexico for J. A.— Ihta—   c/o Mr. Beaton — sent. Fr to Art. I was hurt because he had not sent me the address. Address was written on a blue envelope in left hand corner. [know just how much it would hurt if I got his address from somebody else. In a way I would like to drop the whole deal. Close the account. But Friendly Finance never

---

78. **Auaska** [*sic*], i.e., Ayahuasca, the Quechua name for *yagé* for which Burroughs was searching.

79. **All.** is almost certainly an abbreviation for Allerton.

Page 60

In view of subsequent discoveries in Peru, my ~~previous~~ ^{earlier} conclusions ~~on subject of Yage. are completely invalid and subject~~ Yage subject to drastic alteration.

I made subsequent discoveries ~~in regard to~~ about Yage in Peru in view of which ~~forme~~ earlier conclusions are completely invalid.

certain goods, chattels and services, ~~and packing.~~ including the charges and packing.

[4 LEAVES EXCISED, including facing page to this page][80]

---

80. Four leaves were excised from the notebook following page 60. The excised leaves have not been paginated. Note that it is impossible to determine if the facing pages at the point of excision (see facsimile, pages 60–61) were written as a textual unit, though the editors suspect not.

Page 61

The situation is getting worse. Well this is what you ordered. Isn't it? Some one not [as replaceable] interchangeable.[81] Nothing was said on the contract as to degree of reciprocity: an affair being the only stipulation. So like the Rosenbergs'.[82] "What you have sought have have[83] obtained." Is this the closest you can come to contact? [Approach to complete <u>interchangeability</u> is approach to <u>no</u> contact]. if I[84] can't. No one can. It is precisely <u>your own</u> hyster[85] confusion ~~hys~~ you want to contact. Is in fact part of <u>yourself.</u>

August 3,

Ran into Phil Benton.[86]   Letter to Angelo All over S. A. the dream _____ . ~~I have a feeling~~ Did not show. I have a feeling he is gone too. I'd like to quit, close out A's account. But Friendly Finance never turns loose of a client, or an agent. Contract.

The Party in the first part _____

Pages 62–63

being of the human species, ~~and in condition to~~ does hereby does ~~swear and~~ agree to fulfill the terms of the contract as follows. Clause. 1 – [0 2 1 0 2 0 X] A. ~~It is hereby agreed that for considerations extended by~~ P. Party in first Part – ~~on receipt~~ for [agree, before][87]

---

81. Editorial restoration of erasure: Some one not **as replaceable / interchangeable.**
82. An apparent reference to Ethel and Julius Rosenberg who were executed for treason, June 19, 1953, about a month before Burroughs began his journey.
83. **have have** [*sic*], i.e., **has been**; see fair copy, page 115.
84. contact.] **AI** can't
85. **hyster** [*sic*], i.e., **hysteric**; see fair copy, page 115.
86. **Benton**, q.v. **Beaton**, see fair copy, page 115: each name appears clear in *The Notebook*, but Burroughs may have intended to use the same name in both instances, especially in light of their proximity and context, i.e., Benton's/Beaton's relation to Friendly Finance.
87. Editorial restoration of erasure: Part: ~~on receipt~~ for **agree, before / August 4**

August 4.

No sign of Angelo. He's gone too. ~~It.~~ I hate Mexico, whole fuckin[88] hemisphere. No wonder they took off from S. A. to the South Pacific . Ending up in the worst place of all. Easter Island and the fear of death. Fear of death is form of stasis horrors. The dead weight of time. In East is no stasis horrors because timeless.

Everything is detestable to me. Mexico the rain, everything. Allerton. His sweetness is a fraud, he is a square who

---

Pages 64–65

[All the foriegnors[89] out. Get out expecting suspicious, hostile cop. A pale ghost of a courteous presence in the misty room young Indian writes down the data. "Hay[90] un animal."

H & H face to face across misty, windy gap. Whats[91] the matter with that guy over there? I say you what do you want? I don't know. What do you want. You and Cant[92] you see its[93] impossible? pointing to misty canyon.]

Swallowed the U. S. A. culture con.[94] whole. ~~The~~ A representative of this miserable ~~eu~~ culture ~~sorry~~ hideous with pointless conflict, stupid terrors, a spacho-somatic[95] illness accepted with the cynical resignation of a sick cow. I hate the whole fuckin[96] hemisphere. How typical American to go to bed with some one and resent it at the same time

---

88. **fuckin** [*sic*], i.e., fucking
89. **foriegnors** [*sic*], i.e., foreigners
90. data. "**Hoy** un
91. **Whats** [*sic*], i.e., What's
92. **Cant** [*sic*], i.e., Can't
93. **its** [*sic*], i.e., it's
94. **Swallowed the U. S. A. culture con** is the apparent continuation of the narrative sequence from the end of page 63, **he is a square who**. Bracketed section immediately above appears unrelated to narrative sequence.
95. **spacho–somatic** [*sic*], i.e., psycho somatic
96. **fuckin** [*sic*], i.e., fucking

Pages 66–67

[margin, left:] sickness[99]

and damp and cold, and an shifting

∨ inside — now stomach, now one-day a stomach-ach

Everything has gone wrong here. The question is why did they ever leave in first place? Something like the European immigrant? Land of opportunity, life — room all that shit ? Look at the imigrants[97] who come to America looking for a better life. What they got now. If they had the misfortune to be successful one of the most gruesome cultural strait jackets in history.

[below "strait":] straight

Why the fear of the Foriegnor?[98] The white Foriegnor. All S. A. can pass without papers, but a foriegnor can not.

Last few days in Lima a nightmare The wind across the rubbly lots,[100] and no boys ∧ [101] and the. <u>I have to get out of here.</u>

Pages 68–69

[margin, left:] ∨ on a rising

Last night dreamed of a great ~~black~~ atomic cloud coming up from Chile spreading a

[above "purple":] black

purple shadow over ~~Peru~~ Lima, darker and darker. A boy stands in ^fron^ the violet light, ∧ and throwing a jujo.[102] ~~He~~ and, whistles an insolent little tune. The Chinamen are shutting the doors of their shops, pulling down metal blinds.

A blind legless beggar plays a sad high mountain tune on a bamboo pipe in the empty street.

The reformed drunk, the years of protest over, the circle complete, back ∧^in Indiana^reading a detective story in a lumpy arm chair. ~~an in a little white house in a mid west suburb in Indianapolis a glass of milk~~

---

97. **imigrants** [*sic*], i.e., immigrants
98. **Foriegnor, Foriegnor, foriegnor** [*sic*], i.e., Foreigner, Foreigner, foreigner
99. (margin): **and an** [*sic*] **shifting** appears as **and a shifting** in fair copy, page 116.
100. **rubbly lots** chosen as preferred phrase over muddy lots. Volume editor Oliver Harris notes that "the appearance of the phrase 'rubbly lot' in Burroughs' letter of June 6, 1953, clearly describing the same scene in Lima (and the phrase 'rubble strewn lots' in another version of it), confirms likelihood of" chosen reading.
101. (margin): boys **pride**; boys **outside**
102. A **jujo** may be a misspelling of "juju," a West Africa term meaning amulet or fetish. *The Oxford English Dictionary* says "juju" derives from the French word "joujou," a toy or plaything.

Pages 70–71

The protest has failed. No place to go, ~~the~~ . He packed up and walked out and around in a circle and back. Here he is finally and forever^{soever}[103] here in Indianapolis reading a detective story in a lumpy arm chair. Ouside[104] a November rain and down the street the neon lights of a Bar & Grill.., ~~the cul de sac   that leads back to the arm chair.~~

It's like I came back to Mexico City ~~years~~ after being away 5 years instead of 5 month.[105] Everybody. Gone.

Can visualize Angelo sharp and clear as overdue pusher. His eye brows.   His smile. The way would stop when he saw me with both hands in his pocket his green sweater.

Pages 72–73

His ~~masculine~~ young male gentleness, ~~in that +++ In I felt both an animal serenity.~~

Allerton Gone, Angelo gone. And what have I got? Not even[106] yage.. A visualize[107] a sickness. The memory of places so awful it gives me a ~~sick~~ sinking sensation ~~y~~ to remember myself there. "Naughts[108] had, all's spent." M is almost too pat. Angelo gone. He was the best boy I ever had, and I didn't know it. I used to give him $20. Now I would give him $100. I want to help him. No one else had the same young male gentelness[109] like an affectionate animal. ~~Not a trace of viciousness or conflict.~~ Almost saintly ~~in his~~ in his freedom from viciousness, hostility,

---

103. **soever** [*sic*], i.e., so ever

104. **Ouside** [*sic*], i.e., **Outside**, see fair copy, page 117.

105. **month** [*sic*], i.e., **months**, see fair copy, page 117.

106. **like** yage

107. **visualize** is a best guess by the Editors.

108. **Naughts** [*sic*], i.e., **Nought's**. "Nought's had, all's spent," spoken by Lady Macbeth, Act III, Scene II. Ted Morgan notes in his biography of Burroughs, *Literary Outlaw,* that Burroughs could recall hundreds of quotations of Shakespeare that he was required to memorize in George Lyman Kittredge's Shakespeare course at Harvard.

109. **gentelness** [*sic*], i.e., gentleness

Pages 74–75

conflict.

St-Perse.[110] <u>This is Yage.</u> poetry. Just as there is weed[111] music and painting and poetry.
I wonder if he ever[112] used it. I wonder if it grows in South Pacific.

Ahab has come home. His mistress ~~young wife~~ has ~~gone~~ run off with a traveling
man. His young wife ~~b~~ has gone to ____ with a certain Mr. ____.[113] ~~No one~~ He is
~~regarded~~ avoided on the Bounty by Sailors as an incompetent drunken, lunatic. ~~No one~~
Sure, Jack., the white wale[114] .. "yeah .. Scuse me I got like an appointment"

Outside in the rain. Trainwhistle,[115] and like fog horns, and cars, The City, and ~~I am~~ no
longer

Pages 76–77

have any place here.

What are they talking about Moslem and Christian? Who gives a fuck about religion. I
been to South America. and South Pacific now back here where we started from. all this
is the talk of children. Moslem & Christian! God said. Do they believe all this bull shit
about Allah?

---

110. **St-Perse**, i.e., Saint-John Perse (1887–1975), French poet and winner of the 1960 Nobel Prize for literature. For further
commentary, see "Introduction," pp. xiii–xiv.
111. there is **word**
112. if he **has** used it
113. **man** ____. He is
114. **wale** [*sic*], i.e., whale
115. **Trainwhistle** [*sic*], i.e., Train whistle

Vera Cruz.

Hot and I feel a deep discouragement. My mind goes round and round ~~mechanical~~ repeting[116] the same routine of dull defensive cliches like a nagging idiot. I see the S. A. trip as a disaster that lost me everything I had of value. Bits of it keep floating back to me like memories of a day time nightmare. Slow traps. The

---

Pages 78–79

Mercado Mayorista reveals full gap and indifference by very fact of tolerance. What is wrong with S.A? ~~The~~ Disintegration into component parts. The nightmare[117] fear of death and age, you feel every day as something lost, your flesh ages[118] before your eyes like a speed up movie, Control is growing like a cancer, ~~a like~~ a proliferating ~~growth~~ Tumor of stupidity.

People just disappear. Like in the Mayorista. You never see them again. Angelo.
Here at night people swarm out and walk round and round the square.

The Indians are sad and beaten by the great meaningless country. The New World is a ~~great~~ lack a yearning ache of despair. ~~in~~ deprivation and ~~crippling~~ shrinkage. The fish caught in the shrinking pond

---

116. **repeting** [*sic*], i.e., repeating
117. **nightmare** chosen as preferred term over nighttime. Volume editor Oliver Harris "cannot ever recall Burroughs using the word 'nighttime' whereas the phrase 'nightmare fear' is recurrent (he used it in his 'Yage' letter of June 4, 1953, for example)."
118. **ages** written over aging

Pages 80–81

Dream. I was in Mexico City and ~~each~~ everywhere I looked such an ache of memories of Allerton and people who have gone away. I could not stay there. I must go now too. Angelo sweet and sad, has ~~packed up a~~ gone

away somewhere. ~~I wan~~ The way he used to help around the apt. and he hoped I would help him, and now I want to and he is gone, inexplicably gone like Allerton, and Dave and Jurado, and Juan[119] and all the boys . ~~as if a time gap.~~ ~~had~~ As if I had been away 5 years. I am separated from them by a time gap. and especially from Marker.

Pages 82–83

Merida.[120]

~~Everybody here a mild pain in the ass. They are friendly and sad. Everywhere you~~

~~As though it made thing any better to write about them. Like Liede der Erde Dunkel~~

~~ist en Leben ist der Tod. Yes. Pure lyric only form that has meaning spontaneous as cry~~

~~of pain. Meaning?~~

~~Simply~~

The — lam as he — R. Stern.[121] Why not just hang them? Like in Oran — Is this for my sake?[122] Clyde Gardinier — What is word for Con in Spanish? Gale likes aspirin with codiene.[123] Why. I was sorry then . I don't like abstraction. The reward — homicide squad, by hemp. like Ahab.   John Brown. The white whale — I have[124] lost __. St. Louis

---

119. **Joan** and all the boys
120. **Merida** [*sic*], i.e., Mérida
121. The — lam **and** — R. Stern; The — **law and** — R. Stern; The — **law** as he — R. Stern
122. for my **sore**
123. **codiene** [*sic*], i.e., codeine
124. I **had** lost

Pages 84–85

tragic affairs. Joan. Mrs. Spencer Let it come down[125] — I wunderbar The Last Annals of Rome — Vidal[126, 127] — Damaged to the soul — the news of Marker — Harry — Tom — Dick —

[REMAINDER OF PAGE IS ASEMIC WRITING]

Pages 86–87

[ASEMIC WRITING]

Pages 88–89

[ASEMIC WRITING AND DRAWINGS]

Pages 90–91

[DRAWING]

Pages 92–93

[DRAWING]

---

125. **Let it come down**: The phrase, which derives from *Macbeth,* was also the title of Paul Bowles' 1952 novel.

126. **Vidal**: Gore Vidal's 1948 novel *The City and the Pillar* created a sensation due to its main character being homosexual.

127. Oliver Harris notes that Burroughs had recently been reading new works by these authors and would meet them both within a matter of weeks, in the case of Vidal, in New York, and in a few months, in the case of Bowles, in Tangier.

Pages 94–95

G's gun[128] hide-out — Not much way down yonder in the green field[129] — Missouri cruelty — I'm from Mo, — I gotta be showdby Oh Lord. When I AM HeRE IN this . PLACe Bill, I CAN NOT LeaF PleASe — Do not write Me, BUT COMe Here when yoo Receive this T — AS I Need your professionalAL AttentionAL Kindees of Measure FOR Measure this is A Real bad deal, Bill, I AM CONTIN ON YOUR BONTY MUTINY ON The Bell string Who ever you are now it is timely Aid IN I MUSt HAVe light oR eLSe ?

Pages 96–97

When Lee quit junk — unexpurgated version — First trip to S. A with Allerton. Return to Mexico, Left out — Allerton goes and returns — Back to S. A. No word from Allerton, S. A trip and back to Mexico.

Everything lost —

Pages 98–99

<u>Miami</u> —
Panama —
Colombia —
The horror

---

128. [gun] was erased following **G's** and preceding **hide-out**.
129. the **grave** field; the **grain** field

[DRAWING]

Bogota[130] — Green grass
The Hill — the park —
beggars lined up — Snake Charmer. Spider lal
Back <u>years</u> latter.[131] There is some thing —

L.   B. Lee — In or ✝✝ — blighted — I can not or will not ——

[TWO DRAWINGS]

Pages 100–101

S. A. The giving up. The quiting.[132] The resignation,
                       a little drunk
He got on the plane ~~drunk,~~ his clothes soaked with ~~junk sick sweat~~ [DRAWING]

Panama and old Bill —

Lee

Pages 102–103

Mexico, D. F.

Everybody gone. Old Ike disappeared, Allerton gone, Angelo gone, my lawyer still on the lam. as if I had been away 5 years.

---

130. **Bogota** [*sic*], i.e., Bogotá
131. **latter** [*sic*], i.e., later
132. **quiting** [*sic*], i.e., quitting

about the editors

GEOFFREY D. SMITH is professor emeritus and former head of the Rare Books and Manuscripts Library of The Ohio State University Libraries and adjunct professor in the department of English. He received his doctorate from Indiana University where he first became interested in textual editing through a Textual Studies concentration and work with the *Selected Edition of William Dean Howells.*

JOHN M. BENNETT was born in Chicago. He received his doctorate in Latin American literature from UCLA. A life-long poet, his work started to become well-known in the 1970s. He has worked in a wide variety of genres, including text, visual poetry, graphics, sound and performance poetry, mail art, film and media, and has collaborated with other writers and artists from around the globe. He was also editor of the international literary journal *Lost and Found Times* from 1975 to 2005. He is the founding curator of the Avant Writing Collection at The Ohio State University Libraries.

Specializing in Burroughs scholarship since the 1980s, **OLIVER HARRIS** has edited *The Letters of William S. Burroughs, 1945-1959* (1993), *Junky: the definitive text of "Junk"* (2003), and *The Yage Letters Redux* (2006). The author of *William Burroughs and the Secret of Fascination* (2003) and numerous critical essays, he is professor of American literature at Keele University, England.